# Illumination:

## Spiritual Meditation and Prayer

## Julie Ann Lynch

# To Believers

# Contents

Introduction ................................................7

Meditation 1: The Spirit of Love and Light .............11

Meditation 2: Christ is Love and Light....................12

Meditation 3: God Forgives ...................................14

Meditation 4: God is One God ...............................16

Meditation 5: Eternal God, Source of all Life..........18

Meditation 6: Love one Another .............................20

Meditation 7: God the Giver of Gifts ......................22

Meditation 8: Pray Always.....................................23

Meditation 9: God Lives and Moves in Us ...............25

Meditation 10: Reflect and Magnify God's Love and Light...................................................................27

Meditation 11: Give God our First Fruits...............29

Meditation 12: Unconditional Love ........................31

Meditation 13: God is not Partial...........................33

Meditation 14: The Living Word ............................35

Meditation 15: Beyond the Veil..............................37

Meditation 16: Lord of all Creation........................39

Meditation 17: The Choices We Make ......................42

Meditation 18: Good Stewardship ...........................44

Meditation 19: Invitation to Christ ........................46

Meditation 20: Communion with God ....................48

Meditation 21: Live in the Moment ........................52

Meditation 22: Spiritual Battle and the Problems We Face ......................................................................54

Meditation 23: Free Will is a Sacred Trust.............56

Meditation 24: The Vision Set before Us ................59

Meditation 25: Simplicity a Key to Life ..................62

Meditation 26: Persevere in Faith, Hope, and Love.66

Meditation 27: Roses with Thorns ..........................69

Meditation 28: "Like a Butterfly" The Transformation of the Soul ....................................71

Meditation 29: Focus on what is Good ....................73

Meditation 30: Why so much Suffering? .................76

Meditation 31: Lead by Example ............................82

Meditation 32: The Battle Belongs to God ...............88

Meditation 33: Love Bears Fruits of Peace and Joy.94

Meditation 34: It is God who Calls Us .....................99

**Meditation 35: God hears all Prayer**......................**106**

**Meditation 36: God has a Plan and a Purpose for Us**
...............................................................................**111**

**Meditation 37: Seek the Spiritual Things First**......**114**

**Meditation 38: Life is a Prophecy** ..........................**122**

**Meditation 39: The Communion of Saints** .............**127**

**Meditation 40: Pray through the Gospel**...............**143**

**Epilogue** ...............................................................**158**

# Introduction

This book is an introduction to prayer of the heart. It is written with the intent of taking people from their minds to their hearts. It goes beyond praying a few words from our minds. We are called to come to God with open hearts. He desires to dwell in the hearts of his people.

This book is not meant to teach the literal or historical sense of the Word of God. It is about experiencing the spiritual and allegorical sense of God's Word as it pertains to Christ and his church. This book is a collection of forty meditations and prayers. Forty is a number symbolizing testing and preparation. God is calling us all to prepare our hearts. He is inviting us to dine at his table. We don't know our final day or hour.

I was inspired by the Holy Spirit to write this book based on personal revelation. Personal revelation comes through prayer from the heart, reading the Word, and listening to the Word. Prayer from the heart is an open, receptive awareness to God in every moment. Illumination is to make clear with the light of God. God desires to shine his light on all souls. He wants us to see and hear him with the eyes and ears of our hearts. This is a place where his merciful love meets truth.

This book is written in the plural form, because it is not just about God and you, me, or them, but about God and us. When we pray for all, we pray for ourselves. A few prayers are personalized to make a personal statement of faith. All the prayers can be personalized. God calls his people to be united as one in the Holy Spirit. His house is a place of perfect love and pure light. To pray for others, as we pray for ourselves, is a step toward loving others as ourselves.

This book is written in an extremely simple fashion. God loves all people unconditionally and equally. He desires that all people come to dwell in his house of perfect love and pure light. God reveals to the simple, so that people can understand his words of eternal life. It is best to start from the beginning of this book. It starts with very simple prayers, and finishes with prayers to help us understand more profound mysteries in God.

God is one God. He calls us to be one church united in him through the Holy Spirit. He calls us to selfless and unconditional love. He invites us to freely give, as he freely gives. He desires we all live one day in the perfection of his love.

When reading each meditation, think about what is written. Take time to reflect on, ponder, and contemplate each prayer meditation. When thinking about what you're reading, ask God questions in your heart. Expect God to answer. Take time to truly listen, and be aware when he answers. Ask God to help you pray spontaneously from the heart. Close your eyes and listen. Whatever comes to you, pray it from the heart. This is the beginning to prayer with the heart. Your prayer may be only a few words to start. Eventually the words will flow from your heart, as you grow in God's love and light.

It's not only about thinking it's about knowing. To believe is to know, and to know is to experience. Prayer starts with our thoughts, but to experience the knowledge of God is to go higher than our thoughts. Though God delights in our passionate worship; this is not an emotional experience. Prayer with the heart is an encounter with the Living God. Healing starts with a change on the inside and manifests outwardly. When we learn to pray from the heart the Word will eventually pour out like rivers of living water into the world.

Think of this book as a healing book. Healing of the soul is a gradual transformation. Healing of the body is an outer manifestation of what is taking place on the inside. When our minds are sanctified in truth, and our hearts are emptied of all the emotional baggage, we are filled with the merciful love of God. When our sins are forgiven, we will rise up and walk with God.

When the Word is revealed in my heart it comes to me in a melodic flow; whether written, spoken, or directly taught by God, it is mixed together and flows. I believe the Spirit is calling us to prepare our hearts to meet Christ. This could be in a way we don't think. This is not a scripture study, but messages to pray, turn to God with the heart, and change our ways to his way. We are called to be an example of Christ. In this book, scripture references are for comparison.

When meditating on God's Word and praying, ask God for the grace to see the Word with the heart, so that it becomes life in the soul and manifests outwardly toward others. We can pick up a picture of our loved ones, look at it fondly, and put it back on our nightstand, or we can give them a call or a visit, and converse with them for a while. In this way, we can tell them how much we love them and how much they mean to us. It is the same with God.

Before beginning each meditation and prayer, invoke the Holy Spirit:

*Pray: Holy Spirit of God's pure light, illuminate my mind and heart, and help me to understand each and every prayer and meditation with the heart. Speak to me and teach me; I am listening.*

# Meditation 1: The Spirit of Love and Light

God is Spirit. God is love and light. He lives and moves through all of creation which is wonderfully made. He is present everywhere, to and beyond the ends of the universe. God is perfect love and all-knowing. He longs to abide in the souls of all people. God is neither male nor female, but Spirit. He wills that all creatures move and live in harmony with the Spirit of love and light. The Spirit of love and light longs to embrace us, as a groom embraces his bride.

*Pray: God of the heavens, the universe, the earth, seas, and sky, help us to see your beauty in all things, in nature, and all of creation. Help us all to be thankful and appreciate all that you made good. Sanctify our minds in the light of your knowledge. Purify our hearts with your perfect love. Send your Holy Spirit of universal truth and love into my heart and soul, and the souls of all people. Let us be one in the love and knowledge of your goodness and light. Let there be peace in the hearts of everyone. Let all nations know your everlasting peace.*

*We ask this in the name of the Eternal God of love and light, Amen.*

# Meditation 2: Christ is Love and Light

Christ is Spirit. Christ is the unconditional love of God, and the light of all knowledge. God's knowledge is higher than ours. Christ came in the flesh and gave all. Through the giving of his life, the veil between the physical world and the Kingdom of God was opened. Jesus, Son of God, is perfect in love, and the light of all truth. He died on the cross for all, even his enemies.

He teaches us through the cross to stop being so selfish. We all have a purpose in our life journey on earth. We come from God's Spirit to live, love, and learn. To receive love, we are called to give love. We are to love others as ourselves. The highest love is to give up what we can have for ourselves, for the sake of others.

The Spirit of God loves us unconditionally. To love as God loves, we are to stop putting conditions on others. He calls us to love with his heart, forgiving one another. When we open our hearts to God's love it will flow like a crystal clear stream out toward others. As we ourselves change, the world around us will begin to change. The more we yield to God's presence and love, the more his love will flow out into the world.

*Pray: Eternal Father, thank you for sending Jesus Christ your son to die on the cross, for the forgiveness of sins. Thank you that Jesus is risen from the dead, so whoever believes in him can have eternal life. Christ Jesus, come into my heart and the hearts of all the people on earth. Fill us all with the Spirit of love and the light of all truth. Forgive my sins and the sins of all people. Forgive all who have sinned against us.*

*Flood our souls with your healing presence and love. Be merciful toward us all. Pure River of Life, move through our souls. Wash us clean from the stains and impurities of darkness and death. You bring us healing and life. Show us the way to your highest love. Help us to move, through forgiveness of one another, beyond the veil that separates us from your presence. As we live through, in, and with Christ, let us become conduits of love and light. Let us love and forgive one another, so we may be healed. Guide us all into the light of truth, and bring healing to our souls. May we all live in the harmonies of heaven, and have eternal life forever.*

*We thank you Father, in the name of the Risen Lord, Jesus Christ, Amen.*

## Meditation 3: God Forgives

God loves us and forgives us. In order to receive forgiveness, we need to forgive others and ask for it. He sees true sorrow for sins, and fills our hearts with life. It is God alone who saves us, and determines infinite justice and mercy. God alone is Just Judge. When we judge others, we bring judgment upon ourselves.

In God's mercy there is justice. His perfect love corrects us. We shouldn't blame others for our mistakes. Each day try not to judge. If it happens stop and ask for forgiveness, and stop making excuses. We need to take accountability for what we know is wrong, and ask for forgiveness.

Those who have more are accountable for more. Those who have less are accountable for less. Our place in the kingdom will be determined by how much we love unconditionally. Only God in his pure love and perfect knowledge can see our true motivations. We need to ask God for his light to see with the heart how we are offending him and others. It is through the light of Christ that our consciences can be illuminated, so that we can see with the heart how we need to change.

When others are "pushing our buttons" and annoying us with their idiosyncrasies, we need to look within. When situations anger us and we begin to blame others, we need to forgive and ask for forgiveness. We need to take accountability for our own sins and negative feelings. When we become bitter, anger has taken root in our souls. This "bitter root" will block the healing grace of God in our bodies, minds, and souls.

*Pray: Merciful God, we ask for the grace of unconditional love and pure light. Give us the grace to change, and turn away from all that brought harm to ourselves and others. Help us all to see ourselves in your light, so that we learn what it truly means to love one another unconditionally. You alone are Just Judge. It is you who will determine the measure of justice and mercy you will bestow upon us all.*

*All praise to the God of heaven and earth, and to Christ Jesus, who lives and reigns as one God, in the Spirit of universal love and light, Amen.*

# Meditation 4: God is One God

God is one God. God loved the world so much, that through the Spirit of Christ, the Word of God became flesh in Jesus. Through his life, death, and resurrection, the veil between the physical world and the Kingdom of God was torn. God opened the kingdom of love and light for all who believe. He is the source of all life, love, and light. He longs for all of his people to choose life, love, and light. It is through Jesus sacrifice of himself out of obedience to God the Father, we can move from the physical world into his presence. In dying to our old nature of darkness and sin, we rise to new life in him. Through the resurrection of Christ, we have eternal life in heaven forever. God's kingdom has no end.

The Word and Spirit teaches, as God the Father is one with his Son Jesus and the Holy Spirit of love and truth, he longs for us to become one, as members of the body of Christ. God made us in his image. As members of the body of Christ, we are more than separate parts. We are joined together like pieces of a large puzzle. We are all shaped differently, but joined together by Christ. Though we have different callings and purposes, we are joined together with other members flowing in the harmonies of heaven. Together as one, we are bound by the Spirit of love and light. Our true unity is in Christ.

Jesus is the Word of life. Meditate on the words of Jesus and think about what is true. God desires that his words of life become alive in our hearts. God invites us not only to believe in and receive his words of life, but to become living examples of what we believe. We are not only to serve with words, but with our lives.

*Pray: Eternal God, in you we find the eternal words of life. Pour your words of eternal life into our hearts. Let your word and Spirit of knowledge, life, and love, come alive in us. Your words of truth take us higher than our own thoughts. They give us new freedom and new hope. Help us to see and hear with the eyes and ears of our inner spirit. Renew and restore our souls. Let your thoughts, be our thoughts, and your ways, be our ways. Infuse the perfect love and pure light of Christ into our flesh. Become life in us.*

*All glory and praise to the Eternal God, Jesus Christ the Eternal Word, with the Spirit of love, together as one God, Amen.*

# Meditation 5: Eternal God, Source of all Life

God is eternal, infinite, unlimited, and the source of all life. God existed before the beginning of time, and in him is the origin of all life. He is the Eternal Father of all that is visible and invisible. He is neither male nor female, but Spirit. His people, the church are allegorically called woman, mother, and bride. This helps us understand God's intimate relationship with his people.

God moves all things into being through thoughts and words. The Word is with God and always with God. The Word and Christ Spirit were with God since the beginning. In God all that was; is and is to come. In him all that is; was and is to come. In him what is to come; was and is, because God is I Am. God sees the total picture. He knows all the choices we are going to make before we make them. He knows how he is going to provide a way out for those who love him. He knew us before we were born. Pray always and trust God.

The thoughts and words of God are like a container that brings us perfect love and pure light. Perfect love is unconditional love. It is sacrificing what we can have for ourselves, and giving and sharing what we have with others, for the love of God. Jesus showed us this when he gave up his life for us. He could have gained the whole world, but he didn't. With the love of the Father, he chose us instead, and became the one perfect sacrifice. He desires all to have eternal life in the kingdom of love and light. Pure light is the knowledge of

God, and the beauty and greatness of all he does. Pray for the inner lights of wisdom, knowledge, and understanding.

God Spirit is pure, holy, and power. God sanctifies our minds with his truth, and purifies our hearts with his unconditional love. The Eternal Father desires to clothe us with his power. He sows seeds of truth and love into our hearts. He is Father of all life, and it is his will to fill us with his words of life and perfect love.

When we are clothed with power of Christ and have the indwelling Christ within, we live in God, as he lives in us. We are called out of ourselves and the ways of the world and into the presence of God. The Word and Spirit are a living presence. When we receive his words of life into our hearts, they become life in us. The presence of the living Christ becomes flesh in us. God desires to transfigure us, healing our minds, emotions, and bodies. He calls us to be love, light, and life to a broken world filled with darkness, death, and destruction.

*Pray: Eternal Father, sanctify our hearts and minds with your eternal words of life. Purify our souls with your unconditional love. Let the whole world be filled with your love and your words of life. Come alive in us! Let the words of Christ Jesus become flesh in us. Clothe us and overshadow us with the power of your Holy Spirit. Transform us in body, mind, and spirit.*

*Thank you, in the name of the Eternal Father, the Eternal Word, and the Holy Spirit, one God and true God. Amen.*

# Meditation 6: Love one Another

We come into this world to love and to learn. We are here to learn and experience God's unconditional love. We are called to love God and one another. This includes all, even our enemies. When praying, we shouldn't just pray for ourselves and loved ones, but for all with the same needs. When we pray for all it includes ourselves and our loved ones.

It is good to pray blessings on all people wherever we go. Pray blessings of love, peace, and joy on all. Pray that everyone prospers and finds their purpose in life. When praying for healing, pray for all. When praying for our families, pray for all families.

We are called to give our time and talents from the heart. Those who have the talent of making money should ask God Spirit how to help others. It is good to ask God how to share and bless others with our abundance. All the power to obtain wealth, gifts, and talents comes from God. We all need to take inventory of our own motivations. Are we using God's gifts and talents to build up a kingdom of wealth for ourselves, or are we using God's gifts and talents for the glory of God and to love others? We are in this world for a short time to love, learn, give, and serve. God gives and loves us unconditionally, even when we don't deserve it. What kind of conditions are we putting on others before we will love them, serve them, or give to them?

*Pray: Eternal Father of the heavens, earth, and all that was made visible and invisible, teach us how we can use our gifts and talents to help others. Pour your spiritual blessings upon us all. Bless us with love, peace, and joy. Fill our souls and the whole world with your holy presence. Let peace reign in every soul and every nation. Please meet the temporal needs of all people on earth. Bless us with wealth, food, and housing. We pray for good health for all. Bless all marriages and families in the world. Bless all religious leaders and religions.*

*Grant us understanding of one another. Give us the grace to respect all belief systems. Help us to be a better example of what is good and holy in our own belief systems. Make us all stronger witnesses to your love and truth in this broken world. Heal our souls, heal our bodies, and heal our world. May heaven and earth unite and flow in the perfect harmonies of your kingdom of love and light forever and ever.*

*All glory and praise to you Eternal Father, and to Jesus your Son, and to the Holy Spirit, Amen.*

# Meditation 7: God the Giver of Gifts

We should always be open to whatever gifts and talents God plans to give us. We all have a purpose for being. We need to be open to how God chooses to bless us spiritually and temporally. He desires to meet our needs, and will send us blessings from the Holy Spirit, and through others. Let people receive joy by letting them serve and give to us. When we give, we receive by keeping an open channel to God's abundance flowing.

Always give thanks to God, the font in which all abundant life flows. Selfishness blocks the channel of abundant life. God gives us each gifts to love and serve others. We are to be open channels of love and light to this hurting world. Let us be good stewards of God's gifts and talents by using them to love one another.

*Pray: God of love and light, help us to be good stewards of your wealth and abundance. Show us how to deliver out of the treasures of our hearts, the spiritual and temporal blessings you bestowed upon us. Help us to be open to receive the abundance of wealth, you choose to give us. In turn, let what we receive flow through us out into the world, so that we keep a channel of giving and receiving flowing from your abundance. Let us truly know what it means to love one another. Bless us all with peace, joy, and abundant life.*

*We give all praise and glory to the Father, through the abundant life of Christ Jesus, together with the Spirit of life, Amen.*

# Meditation 8: Pray Always

Pray always, unceasingly in God's Spirit. Focus on the light, walk in the light, and live in the light. God calls us to come to him with open hearts, with sorrow for all the pain and suffering, we brought into this world and the lives of others. It is necessary to forgive others to receive forgiveness. He invites us to come to him with an open, receptive awareness of his presence in every situation. God is present in the visible and the invisible. He calls us to be mindful of him everywhere we go and in whatever we do. He invites us to be aware of both his indwelling presence and his presence that surrounds us all.

God is everywhere. He is sovereign over all the heavens, earth, seas, and sky. He is larger than the universe. He is universal truth and love. He holds all things together and calls all things into being. He calls us by name. He knows all and sees all. He is aware of all things good and bad.

Spend time meditating on the truth. Invoke the presence of the Holy Spirit. Ask to experience the love and knowledge of God. Just be still, be quiet, and listen. To pray always, doesn't just mean vocal prayer. To pray is a two way conversation with God.

He invites us to step out of ourselves into an awareness of his presence. Take time to notice random occurrences. These things are no coincidence. God speaks to us through prayer, his word, through books, in nature, and through other people. Try to be aware of him in all situations. God is trying to get our attention, learn from him. Our mistakes and sufferings can be a learning experience. Give them to God.

We are called to make our life a prayer to God. We are not only called to prayer with words, but with our lives. When we make our lives spiritual worship, our prayers become life and our lives become a prayer. Prayer from the heart rises like incense, a sweet fragrance of life pleasing to God. He would like to see all souls blossom like a rose, turning toward the sun, with the sweet fragrance of Christ's life within.

*Pray: Eternal Father, Creator of heaven and earth, help us to be aware of your presence in all things, situations, and moments in time. Help us to see and hear you with the eyes and ears of our hearts. May we notice your promptings, whether they come in a gentle breeze or a raging storm. Let us hear your voice in the stillness of our hearts. Surround us all with your light, beauty, and power. In the quiet of our beings help us to hear your peaceful voice. Teach us your ways, so that we may walk with you all the days of our lives.*

*We thank you Father, in the name of Jesus, Amen.*

# Meditation 9: God Lives and Moves in Us

God lives and moves through us, with us, and in all who believe. He calls us to faith. He not only invites us to believe, but to live what we believe. God loves us, reaching out to us like a loving parent. Many people have never experienced the love of God. This is the greatest hunger of the human heart. Once people taste the love of God, they are satisfied with nothing less than his love. He calls us to be his hands and voices in the world.

When praying ask the Holy Spirit how to help others. We might be the only witness of God's presence a person might see or hear. When we are filled and surrounded by God's love and light, our countenances will radiate like the sun. We will bring warmth to others embracing them with Christ's light. Don't just talk about peace, love, and joy, but become these things so others will believe and be healed. God calls us to be a life-giving spirit of love, so others will be inspired to choose life.

*Pray: Heavenly Father, make your children on earth a channel of life-giving water, so all who thirst may drink. Let your river of life flow through us in purity and unconditional love. Set us free from the pollution of darkness, death, and sin. Remove the clogs from our spiritual pipes, and the dams of clutter that block the free flow of your living water. Let us all be open conduits of your love and power, to help heal a broken world. Most of all help us to truly know what it means to love one another, as you love us. Fill our hearts today with overflowing love, peace, and joy. Thank you Father, with great appreciation for all the great works you have done for us and through us.*

*We pray this with all glory, praise, and thanksgiving to the Father, to the Son, and to the Holy Spirit, Amen.*

# Meditation 10: Reflect and Magnify God's Love and Light

God not only calls us to reflect the light of Christ, but to magnify his light, fire, and love over the whole earth. God calls us to shine in his radiant light, splendor, and presence. God's love is like a fire that burns away all that doesn't belong to his perfect love and pure light. Like pure gold in fire, he removes our impurities. He shapes us like beautiful gems that sparkle in the magnificent splendor of his beauty. God calls us out of darkness and death into light and life, shining like a full moon on a clear night. God shines his light into the deep darkness of our souls, transforming us like a new moon with no visible light, to a full moon, a reflection of the great and radiant splendor of the sun. Though we may not have natural beauty, our countenances will shine with the light of Christ.

*Pray: Eternal God of universal love and light, pour your Spirit of love and light into our hearts and minds. Refine us as gold in fire, washing away sin and darkness and removing impurities. Shine the light of the Son on us all. Let all the earth enjoy your beauty and splendor. Through Christ, rise us up out of darkness and death into new life. Renew us all, and shape us into the character of Christ. Let us all live and walk in his ways. Let our countenances radiate and our souls magnify, the light and fire of the Son.*

*We give all the splendor and glory to God the Father, Son, and Holy Spirit, Amen.*

# Meditation 11: Give God our First Fruits

We should offer up to God our hearts, minds, and our total beings every day, giving our first fruits to God every morning, first thing upon waking. Pray unceasingly all day, with God awareness, rising up out of ourselves into the presence of the Holy Spirit. Seek the presence of God in all things and circumstances. When we remain in sin, our countenances will fall and not radiate the light of Christ Spirit. Sins rooted in deadly sins such as; anger, lust, greed, envy, sloth, gluttony, and pride (cf. 1Jn. 5:16), (cf. Catholic Catechism 1866), will keep us trapped in an earthly existence. Also fear, judging others, selfishness, and unwillingness to forgive, will keep us imprisoned in darkness.

Moving beyond the veil and into the presence of God requires prayer with faith, repentance, and obedience to God's will. Obedience to God proves love and counteracts pride. To live in the will of God, is to live in his love. Grace is God's unconditional love. He calls us to live in a state of grace. Always be slow to anger, forgive, don't blame anyone, and judge no one, and the blessings will flow in the harmonies of heaven.

*Pray: Lord God of heaven and earth, I offer up my heart to you today. Please fill my heart with your grace and mercy. Pour your grace and mercy into all hearts, bringing conversion of all sinners. I offer you my total being, my heart, my soul, and strength. Make my life a pleasant offering, pleasing to your senses. Forgive all my sins, as I forgive all those who have offended me. Be merciful to us all, so that we may all be an offering to you, in the unity of the Holy Spirit.*

*I ask this in the name of the Merciful Savior, Jesus Christ, Amen.*

# Meditation 12: Unconditional Love

God calls his faithful people to go out into this world with a grateful heart, to be light and mercy to a broken world. He asks us to love others, as he loves us unconditionally. He asks us to love and bless others without putting conditions on them. God loves us all, even if we do nothing to deserve it. He calls us to pray and seek how we should reach out and bring comfort to the lost, poor, sick, and lonely. We are to be light to those living in darkness and depression, reaching out to them with mercy and love.

We are not to just prophesy with our lips, but with our lives. Our lives should be a sweet smelling fragrance to God. Give affection and love; bless people with peace and joy. We are to be an example of life, peace, and the joy of Christ. Through faith we are justified. Faith opens the door to the kingdom of infinite possibilities. Our place in the kingdom will be determined by how much we love, because God is love. This is not emotional love, but a higher love that loves not only our friends, but those who are difficult to love.

*Pray: God of abundant love, fill our hearts with love, peace, and joy to overflowing. Let your rivers of life flow through us, and your joy and peace well up in us so much that we bring your joy and healing to all. Give us the grace to love unconditionally, as you love us. Transform our minds and hearts in your pure light and perfect love.*

*Thank you Father of Love, in the name of Christ our Lord, Amen.*

# Meditation 13: God is not Partial

God is not partial, but loves all equally and infinitely. He wills that all his people on earth share in the bounty of his kingdom. Through faith, we receive grace, his unconditional love, and mercy. Through faith we are justified, and the doors of heaven are open to us. It is God's people on earth that divide on matters of faith. Through true sorrow for sins, we receive mercy and forgiveness; this is a key to life. When we truly believe, we will be truly sorry for our sins. The wages of faith and true sorrow for sins is eternal life for all who believe. When we are justified by faith, God's grace sanctifies us from our sins.

God's kingdom is love, which he builds in the hearts of his people. Each one of our choices that line up with the will of God takes us closer to him. Our battle is not with each other, but with spirit. When we make choices contrary to the will of God, we can find ourselves battling with God. Each one of our choices that line up with God's will takes us higher on the ladder to paradise. God's kingdom has levels of glory, in which he transforms us through each choice we make, because of love.

In the Father's house there are many dwelling places. Our place in his house is determined by the state of our souls. It is determined by how much we loved God in spiritual worship, and how much we loved others unconditionally, including our enemies. We will be judged by how much we are truly sorry for the harm we brought to others and the earth. The more a soul reflects the love and light of God, the more beautiful it becomes.

*Pray: Lord God, Heavenly Father, may all souls on earth reflect the beauty and splendor of your glorious love and light. Give us all the grace and light to see the light of truth in our hearts. Illuminate our consciences with your light. Let your sword of light pierce our souls and fill all hearts with peace and joy to overflowing. Give us all the grace to make righteous choices in life. Transform us in your image through Christ Jesus. Let the inner character of Christ be our inner character, so that we may all be a people of unity in the Spirit of love. Make us all children of the light, so that your light pierces the darkness of deception and death.*

*We ask this in the glory of the Father, through Christ our Lord, Amen.*

# Meditation 14: The Living Word

The Word was made flesh in Christ Jesus, and in the flesh, he is the Living Word of God. God wills his words of life to become life in our flesh, so that we become examples of Christ. He desires to infuse his life, presence, and total being into our hearts, minds, souls, and bodies, so that his entire life becomes life in our flesh. He desires to assimilate his being with our being, so that his heart, mind, and flesh become one in us all, uniting us all in the glory of the Father. We are all partakers of the same loaf of bread (cf. 1Cor. 10:17), joined by the leaven of Christ's pure light and perfect love.

Words and thoughts have power to bring about realities. We will all be accountable for our words and thoughts that brought darkness into the world. Let all of our words be life, love, and hope, and let all of our thoughts be pure holy light. God knows all of our thoughts and sees all of our hearts. We need to come to God and ask for forgiveness, for all of the words and thoughts that brought harm, suffering, and darkness into our lives, and the lives of others.

*Pray: All-knowing God of truth and light, let our thoughts be perfected in your light, and let our words be truth and life. Send your sword of light into the minds and hearts of all people. Forgive us for the words and thoughts that brought harm and suffering into the world, our own lives, and the lives of others. Let the Word become life in our flesh. Bring unity to us all, in the glory of our Father.*

*We give thanks to you Father, in the name of Christ Jesus, Amen.*

## Meditation 15: Beyond the Veil

God calls us to come to him with open, repentant hearts, with true sorrow, for all the things that we did, and failed to do that we know are wrong. When we respond to his call, he changes our hearts, and molds us into his image, restoring our souls. God reveals to those who come to him with a great big K.I.S.S. (keep it simple souls). He invites us to come to him like children, with simple hearts, honesty, and dependency on him. When praying, ask God questions, and take time to listen, going beyond thoughts and words.

He calls us to a place beyond the veil where we meet him in his presence. This is where the Spirit begins to pray in us, in the flow of the heavenly river of life. The fruits of this type of prayer are incredible peace and joy. It is a taste of heaven while we still live on earth. Don't get discouraged if you don't experience this right away. God sees your heart, and hears all prayer; stay faithful; he's doing a good work in you. There is great beauty in a soul that seeks to see God with the heart.

*Pray: Heavenly Father, I come to you with an open heart ready to receive all the love and mercy you choose to pour into my soul. Be merciful and protect me from sin, darkness, and death. Melt my hardened heart, and forgive me for all the wrongdoings and offences I've committed toward you and anyone.*

*God of mercy and love, bring us all into the light of your presence. Mold us into your image, and restore us in your likeness. Help us all to go beyond our own thoughts and words, into a place where we meet, beyond the veil of the natural, visible world. Speak to us, for we are listening with the ears of our hearts. Let your river of life flow in our souls. Fill us with the peace and joy of heaven. Help us to step out of ourselves and taste heaven on earth. Let the whole earth be filled with your glorious presence.*

*We thank you Father, in Jesus' name, Amen.*

# Meditation 16: Lord of all Creation

God is Lord of all creation visible and invisible. He is higher, deeper, and greater than we can imagine. In God all things move and are called into being. In his perfect will, all things flow like a beautiful melody, a sweet song to his ears. Souls in line with the harmonies of heaven's song are most pleasing to God.

When things get out of balance and harmony, we have moved, not God. We have a way of moving toward the things we think about. Words and thoughts have energy and power. With our words, we can prophesy realities and bring the things we fear into our lives. Surrendering our fears to God, praying, and strong faith can counteract our fears, by placing our trust in God. God calls us to focus on things that are good, holy, and righteous. He can bring a greater good out of any situation. He permits adversity when he can see a greater good.

We are wonderfully made in God's eyes. Wherever we are and wherever we go, it is good to pray blessings on everyone. Bring a smile, joy, and peace to all. When we ourselves change and pray for all, our external lives will begin to heal, and we will move toward a more blessed life. God wills that we taste his joy and peace on earth, as it is in heaven.

When God draws us into his love, the experience can be overwhelming, but once we taste this, nothing else will ever satisfy us. God is uniting heaven and earth;

pray that all souls flow in the harmonies of heaven. We need to prepare our souls by turning away from all that we know is wrong and asking for forgiveness. We need to ask God how to use our blessings, gifts, and talents, to bless others with prayers and deeds. Whatever we do to others, we do to God.

Many of our external trials and sufferings are a result of our choices on earth. These trials and tribulations can start on the inside of us, in our own souls. When we change on the inside, it can begin to manifest with the external healing of our bodies and the external circumstances in our lives. Changing now can heal past mistakes and can lead to a brighter future. God allows us to eat the fruits of our own choices.

We ask God why he allows so much suffering; he asks us the same thing. We are his body, hands, and voices on earth. Let us get moving in our thoughts, words, prayers, and deeds. Let our prayers and words become life, and our lives become a prayer, pleasing to God. External healing is a sign that something greater is going on inside of us. This starts with each and every individual soul, making a decision to become examples of the righteousness, peace, and joy of Christ's eternal love.

*Pray: God of Eternal Love, Creator of all that is visible and invisible, let our prayers be a sweet song rising up to you, so that we may flow in the harmonies of your eternal love. Give us the grace to focus on the beauty of your kingdom of light, love, peace, and joy. Bless us and the whole world with prosperity, peace, and joy. Cleanse our souls with your mercy, and renew us with your Word and Spirit. Send your healing power upon us all, so that we may be healed in our bodies, minds, and souls. Our greatest passion is to do your will above all else.*

*We thank you Father, in the name of Jesus, Amen.*

# Meditation 17: The Choices We Make

It is good to be aware of our choices at all times, in every moment. We should think about whether we are making life choices or death choices. Contemplate whether each choice will bring life, peace, joy, and happiness or whether it will bring suffering, death, or sorrow. We need to consider how our choices will affect ourselves and others. Right choices in the present can lead to a better future and heal past mistakes. Seeking the center of God's will and living in his presence every moment can change nature.

When we become open vessels to God's light and love the world around us begins to change. True peace and joy are not dependent on external circumstances, but exists in the midst of the greatest adversity. We should ask the Holy Spirit, if we are making the right choices. Always follow inner knowing and peace, and the guidance of the Holy Spirit, not anger, anxiety, or fear. If we all did this, the world would begin to heal and nature would come into a greater balance.

The choices we make right now not only affect our own lives and the lives of those around us, but can affect future generations. When the choices bring suffering and death, we will face the consequences of our choices. When we make a decision to change, we not only begin to heal the present, but we bring healing to the past. When we make choices that result in suffering, loss of life, or property, our lifeblood can spill out. Our lifeblood is the love and light of Christ.

Our choices contrary to the will of God can lead to a spiritual state of dark depression and anxiety. Our choices can block the flow of God's grace in our lives. Bad choices can lead to hell on earth for many souls. When people make harmful choices, they justify their choices as good and right choices. This is why we need to ask God to illuminate all consciences, and shine his light into the minds and hearts of all people.

God forgives all sins; ask for forgiveness with a sorrowful heart. We need to forgive others, so he can forgive us. God will restore our hearts, minds, and souls, and lift us out of the pit of darkness, depression, death, and destruction. If we don't forgive, we can stay trapped in a state of darkness and depression, living in a state of spiritual blindness. When we forgive, God will forgive us and renew our souls, so the life-giving water will flow again, as we reconcile with God and one another.

*Pray: God of mercy and forgiveness, you put before us life choices and death choices; give us the grace to make righteous choices in our lives. Give us the light to see your truth through the eyes of the Spirit. Illuminate our consciences, and renew our souls with your merciful love. Let your life-giving water flow in our souls, as you restore us in your image. As you transform us, strengthen our faith and deliver us from anxiety and fear. Help us to be slow to anger, as we grow in compassion for all in need. May the whole world flow and live in your abundant life.*

*All praise and glory belong to you Almighty God, through Christ our Lord, Amen.*

# Meditation 18: Good Stewardship

Where much is given, much is expected; where less is given, less is expected. Those who have more will be accountable for more, and those who have less will be accountable for less. All we have belongs to God; he calls us to be good stewards of all the gifts and blessings he bestows upon us. God's providence is bountiful, beyond measure, his bounty is unlimited. Stop thinking about there not being enough; God is more than enough. He is greater than any situation. The more we pour out, the more we will receive, to be poured out again.

We need to empty out our vats of spiritual and temporal blessings. If we do this, we will be filled to overflowing in the abundant life of God. His wellspring never runs dry. He calls us to give away what we don't need, and share all that we have with joy. When we can, we should try to give back what we take. If everyone lived like this, the world would be a better place.

God provides all of our needs from his abundance. Surrender all things to God; this requires trust. Storing and hoarding indicate a lack of trust. Those who live in complete trust can stand in the middle of the deserts of life and watch God provide. God does not abandon us. God entrusts us with many gifts. These gifts are to be delivered out toward others in need, according to God's purpose. We should pray to the Holy Spirit about how our gifts can be delivered out toward others.

When we live in the center of God's will, we live in the place where all blessings flow. Christ is the fountain of all life, from which all blessings flow. Get into the flow of giving and receiving. This is like a vortex that gets bigger and bigger, the more we love and seek the light of truth. Our abundance, spiritually and temporally flows in from God, and then flows out from us toward God and others. This is the abundant life. In this place, we don't worry about what we need. When we focus on God's perfect will, we live in the center of his providence. When we seek the spiritual things first, in the kingdom of righteousness, peace, and joy, we live in the flow of giving and receiving. In this place we don't give to get; we just live in the flow of giving and receiving, while focusing on Christ.

*Pray: God of wonder beyond all imaginations, your infinite glory is so great that we can hardly contain it. We surrender all things to the center of your will, trusting in your providence. Show us all how to use our gifts and bounty to help and serve others. Take us to the place where all blessings flow. As we seek the light of truth, help us to love with the compassion of Christ. Move through our souls Holy River of life, so that we become life-giving to all that we meet.*

*We pray this prayer, with all praise and thanksgiving to the Father of Life, through Christ the Fountain of Life, Amen.*

# Meditation 19: Invitation to Christ

God calls us to invite the Light of Christ into our hearts. As Christ was born in a dark cave used for animals, God wills to shine his light of truth into the deepest, darkest recesses of our hearts. His will is to wash away all darkness with his living waters of life, so that we can see the light of truth, through our spiritual eyes. God wills to cleanse us from all our sins and past mistakes, with his most merciful love. In the very core and center of our beings, God desires to make his resting place. When we receive Christ Jesus into our hearts, we become new creations in Christ. When we connect our inner spirit with Christ Eternal, we will begin to find our purposes in life. When we begin to find our purposes in life, we move toward a more blessed life in Christ; a place where all things are possible.

We are blessed, to be a blessing to others. It is God who measures out which blessings we are to receive. It is God who chooses us; the Father draws us to him through faith in the Living Word of God. The Living Word of the Father is his Son Jesus, and by the power of Christ, the Spirit of love and light, they are bound together as one true God. It is God's will that we all receive the Word of Life and his merciful love.

It is God's perfect will that all souls would spend eternity with him forever. He always respects our free will not to choose eternal life. If we want eternal life, we need to choose it through Jesus Christ our Lord. Jesus, the only begotten Son of the Father, is the Living Word of God who contains and expresses all love, life, and truth. The Holy Spirit is the power of Christ life, love, and light. They live and reign together as three persons in one true God.

*Pray: Eternal Father, you are the source of all love and light. Pour the Living Word of God into my heart through Christ Jesus my Savior, so that through his cross and death, I will have the forgiveness of sins, and through the resurrection of Christ, I will inherit eternal life. Sanctify my mind in the light of truth, and purify my heart with your merciful love. Forgive all of my sins. Wash me clean in your merciful love, given to us by the shedding of your blood. Let the inner light of Christ shine in my soul, so others will see the glorious presence of God. As I die to my own pride and selfishness, I ask to rise with Christ into new life, in the eternal kingdom of love and light.*

*I pray this in the name of the Father, the Son, and the Holy Spirit, Amen.*

# Meditation 20: Communion with God

When we have communion with God, in the Spirit of love and light, we take on the mind and heart of Christ. God wills that our minds be sanctified in all truth, and our hearts be purified with his merciful love. Jesus showed us on the cross, it is in dying to ourselves that we receive and live the life of Christ. God calls us to take on the mind of Christ, so that his thoughts and ways become our thoughts and ways. God calls us to grow in the inner character of Christ, which is a heart of righteousness. The Word and Spirit teaches us the fruits of Christ's heart are love, peace, joy, gentleness, faithfulness, generosity, kindness, patience, and self-control (cf. Gal. 5:22-23).

Jesus is alive, he is risen; he wills that his presence becomes flesh in our flesh. His presence transforms our souls and transfigures our bodies. The Word and Spirit teaches us, we are partakers of the same loaf (cf. 1Cor. 10:17). When the leaven of sin is removed from our hearts by his merciful love, given to us by the shedding of his blood, we live as consecrated members of the body of Christ. God makes us a consecrated host in the Spirit of unity; Jesus is our new leaven. As there is one loaf, in which we all partake, there is one body in Christ (cf. 1Cor. 12:12-13). In this, all the believers in heaven and on earth are united with him in the Holy Spirit.

In this infusion of the Risen Christ, we take on his mind, heart, soul, and flesh. We are being transformed in his image, when we receive his presence and his words of life into our hearts and minds. This is healing to our souls, which can manifest in greater strength and healing in our bodies, for those who have strong faith and firmly believe. As our souls are nourished, we will begin to see change in our countenances and our external lives. As we share in his sufferings, we share in his resurrection glory; his wounds heal our wounds.

We are called to grow toward the perfection, as we are transformed in the image of Christ. We are called to be sanctified temples of the Holy Spirit, more precious than the finest wood, linens, and precious metals. As we become washed in the water of the Word and the blood of his merciful love, the fullness of Christ becomes more present in our hearts and our lives. His portrait is painted in our hearts, as we become more alive in him. The living Christ becomes known in us.

To know Christ is to experience Christ. This is a love relationship. To understand this relationship, look to Mary, the mother of Jesus. As God is Father, Mary is our mother and Jesus is our brother; as Jesus is her Son, Mary is the daughter of Israel; and as Jesus became man, Mary is woman. The Holy Spirit overshadowed her as her spouse, and the church is clothed with the power of God. The new Adam, Jesus was born from Mary's womb; and the church was born from the blood and water that flowed from Jesus' side and manifested in the flesh of his disciples at Pentecost. Who is the new Eve? As we become sanctified and purified in the light and love of God, we are making ourselves ready for Christ our groom. The church is the holy bride of Christ, who bears the presence of Christ throughout the world.

Christ invites us to offer up our hearts, minds, and souls to him, so that we can be transformed in the likeness of the Risen Lord of life. He calls us to be one in him, as he is one in our Father. We are all individuals with different personalities, gifts, and talents. We are like stones with different shapes, but we are held together by the mortar of the same Holy Spirit of light and love. This is why when we pray for all, we pray for ourselves. When we have communion with Jesus, we have communion with the holy ones in the body of Christ. God invites us all to receive the Risen Christ, so that we become one in him, as he is one in the Father. We are members functioning uniquely by the same Spirit.

In the Lord's last Supper, Jesus did not just pray with words, but with his life. He asks the same of us in remembrance of him. God wants us all to be living stones for his glory, building his house in Spirit and truth. God is uniting heaven and earth, in which all souls should prepare through Holy Communion with God and one another. This is the fulfillment of the kingdom of love, bearing fruits of righteousness, peace, and joy in the Holy Spirit.

*Pray: Heavenly Father, you are the source of all life. Infuse the presence of the Risen Lord into our bodies, hearts, minds, and souls. Remove all the stains of our sins and bring forth the character of Christ in our hearts. Sanctify our minds with the words of life, removing the thorns of pride, sins, and negative thoughts. Give us all your crown of light, so that our consciences are illuminated to see you with the eyes of our hearts. Make our flesh a holy consecrated temple, worthy to receive you.*

*Let our souls be lifted up in the fire of your holy love. Let our souls be healed and filled with the sweet fragrance of your sanctity. Christ Jesus, come alive in us. Reveal to us the Holy Face of the Father in heaven. Send your swords of light and arrows of love to pierce our minds and hearts with the love and knowledge of Christ. Let heaven and earth unite in the Spirit of love and the light of truth.*

*We make this prayer in the name of the Father, the Son, and the Holy Spirit, Amen.*

# Meditation 21: Live in the Moment

God calls us to live in the moment, knowing that whatever happens was already foreseen by God. Accept God's will, as it is right now. In God's plan for us, he permits adversity when he can see a greater good. He can bring good out of any adversity. He knows all the choices we will make before we make them. He knows the end of the story. If we have faith and persevere, God will continue to pour his love and mercy into our hearts.

Surrender all things to God and trust him, one day at a time. Patient waiting builds hope, and as we hope, he builds inner character, as he continues to pour his perfect love into our hearts. When we can't feel him, he is closer than we think. It is God that gives us the desires of our hearts and puts visions before us. He calls us to persevere toward the visions he sets before us. We should ask for God's grace every day to sustain us. Pray to the Holy Spirit for the grace to change what we can, blaming no one. It is what it is for a reason, a purpose, and a season. Rejoice in good times and bad; God is always with us.

We need to take responsibility for the things we do that we know are wrong. He is merciful to forgive, and calls us back to him when we fall away. God knows us and the choices we will make before we are in our mother's womb. We are in this world on a temporary sojourn. We come from God, and he is constantly calling us back to him. Our life in this world is short, while heaven is eternal. If we choose Christ, we will live forever in the kingdom of love and light.

*Pray: Father of Mercy, it is through and in the Spirit of Christ that we live, move, and breathe. Give us the grace we need to persevere in hope toward the visions you set before us. Let all your people on earth receive your graces of mercy, love, and knowledge, to persevere through all the trials you permit in our lives. We believe that you will always provide a way out for those who trust you and come to you in faith, with open hearts. Help all your faithful to persevere in faith and hope, so that you can build your kingdom of love in our souls. It is you Father, who puts your desires into our hearts and minds; make your desires, the desires of our hearts.*

*We ask this in the name of the Father of Eternal Love, and Christ Jesus, together with the Spirit of love, one God forever, Amen.*

# Meditation 22: Spiritual Battle and the Problems We Face

Every problem we face can be a stepping stone to something greater or higher. God calls his children to do great things for him. He permits problems so we can learn from them. Our life mistakes can be a learning experience. When the doors seem to slam shut on things we have been doing for a long time, we need to look for new opportunities. We need to listen to and learn from our highest and greatest teacher, the Holy Spirit who guides us in all truth. God can provide a way out of any situation. His ways and knowledge are far greater than ours.

In order to live in Christ, we need to die to ourselves. God elects those who are rejected. He rises up those who are rejected for higher callings and purposes. God closes doors when he has better plans for us. Persevere in doing what is right and good. There is Good News for all the rejected, the little people, the humble, and the scorned, sitting in the back seat of life. It is God who moves those who are rejected to the front seats for higher purposes. Remember, when feeling rejected, in God we are elected. Situations can seem darkest right before a breakthrough.

*Pray: Almighty God of power and love, help us all to see the higher purposes and callings in and through the problems we face each day. Help us not to see our problems as failure, but a valuable lesson. Help us to see what we can learn from our sufferings. Open the doors to new opportunities in your timing and your way, as we persevere in doing what is right and good. We trust in you.*

*Strengthen our faith, as we wait patiently in you. Help us to be more aware of the promptings of the Holy Spirit. Make your higher ways our ways. We pray for the gifts of knowledge and wisdom. We believe you can bring a greater good from every problem we face. Let the lessons we learn be help and consolation to others going through the same problems and sufferings. Let us love one another, encourage one another, and uphold one another. Let the love and blessings you pour into our hearts and lives, pour out toward others.*

*We give all the glory and praise to you Eternal Father, through Christ our Lord, Amen.*

# Meditation 23: Free Will is a Sacred Trust

We have different measures of truth, love, and understanding. God's love is unfailing, beyond measure. His truth is like a vast ocean of infinite possibilities. All things are possible with God. He gives us free will to make choices. Everything belongs to God except our free will.

We are all unique with different purposes, in God's perfect plan. Each and every one of us has the right to our points of view. It is God's will that we respect the points of view of others, and not try to push our understandings and ideas on them. He calls us to invite others to embrace his kingdom of love and light. We should not try to force others to agree with our words, but become examples of what we believe. When we say we believe in peace, we need to become examples of peace. Do not let others provoke us to anger. Be slow to anger and pray for peace. When we say we believe in life, we should become life-giving to others. It is the Spirit of Christ that gives life; pray for eternal life in Christ for all people.

God puts before us life and death; his will is that we choose life. Whenever we sin, we make death choices. Seek a life free from sin and darkness. When we call ourselves pro-life, we better respect all life, including our enemies. When we say we believe in family values and sanctity in marriage, we need to pray that our own families are healthy and functional. When we say we believe in helping the poor and fair wages, we should be an example of generosity, according to the measure God measures out to us. Pray for, bless, and love all people, with compassion and a desire that all people share in the abundant life of God.

When we cause pain, suffering, and destruction against people, nature, and property, we make death choices. God wills that we all turn away from darkness, death, and sin toward a life in the Spirit. The more we change and become givers of life, love, and light, the more others will respond to God's call. The world will begin to change around us, one soul at a time. We need to pray and ask the Holy Spirit for the grace to change; true change starts on the inside.

Our free will is a sacred trust from God. It is contrary to God's nature to oppress the free will of others. If people make harmful choices there will be consequences in this life and the next. Though there needs to be laws to guide and protect people, property, and nature, laws don't change people. Only the Holy Spirit of grace, mercy, and life can change people, if they are willing to change.

We are called to be examples of light, life, and love to a broken world. Peace and joy are fruits of God's love. When we give love to others through prayers, words, and deeds, the fruits of our works will be peace and joy. We are called to pray for peace for ourselves and the whole world. There are people in the world who have never experienced God's love. Once we taste the love of God, we are satisfied with nothing less than his love. Pray that all people turn away from darkness, death, and sin toward the kingdom of love, light, peace, and joy. God wills that his kingdom be built in the hearts of all, so that not one soul will perish.

*Pray: Eternal Father of love, life, peace, and joy, may all people taste the joy and peace that comes through your love. Pour your love and mercy into our souls, so that we can make righteous choices in our lives. Forgive us all for the choices we made in darkness that brought pain and suffering into the lives of others and the world. Help us to forgive all those who have hurt us. Let us all live together in true peace and harmony, in the image and likeness of our Savior, Christ Jesus. Let us bring the sweet fragrance of Christ life to others, so that their souls will be healed.*

*All the glory and power belong to our Father in heaven, in Jesus' name, Amen.*

# Meditation 24: The Vision Set before Us

It is good to write down the visions that God places into our hearts. We should meditate on his plans for us frequently, keeping the visions he sets before us. God reaches into the deepest recesses of our hearts and sees our desires. He longs to give us the desires of our hearts, which he places there, according to his purpose. We all have a purpose for being. All that is good comes from God. He desires we use our gifts to love and serve others. We can choose to use our gifts for ourselves, or we can use our gifts to love our neighbor, as we love ourselves. Our neighbor includes all people, even those we don't like. God's love is unselfish and unconditional.

We should surrender all our visions to God, his ways are perfect ours are not. There is a reason for everything; sometimes the Spirit's direction in our lives doesn't make sense. When we wander off his straight and narrow pathway, he draws us back. He can make all things good by teaching us his ways from every mistake we make. His ways are perfect, ours are not. We should follow and accept God's plans; there are reasons for everything. God's plans are grander than ours; he sees and knows everything. We cannot conceive what God has prepared for us. His ways are higher than ours.

We should practice God awareness in all things. Live with an open, receptive awareness of God's presence; be aware of him in every present moment. He calls us to pray unceasingly, in the awareness of his presence. When we live in the center of God's will, we will have peace and joy even in the midst of suffering. We need to meditate on the visions God sets before us, letting go of trying to figure out how he is going to fulfill his plans. We need to let go of our own ways of doing things. Always follow the guidance of the Holy Spirit. When we do, we will have peace.

We should try not to let obstacles, frustrations, doubts, and fatigue consume our thoughts. Always resist being consumed with anger and anxiety. God is in control. Life in this world is full of trials and challenges, surrender everything to God, trusting he will provide a way out. It's good to write down solutions and good outcomes to our trials, letting God handle them. Offer them up to God, with faith and trust; this will lead to greater peace and joy in our lives. When we are feeling anxious, we need to ask God to show us how we need to change; this change starts in our hearts.

*Pray: Holy God, Creator of heaven and earth, I surrender all my visions to you. Let all of us have peace and joy, as we move toward the visions you place before us. Let your thoughts and desires become our thoughts and desires. Lord, pour your healing love into our hearts, minds, and bodies. Fill us with your holy light.*

*Give us the strength to remain faithful to you, as you are to us. We pray for the grace to change on the inside, so that our winding paths of pride and selfishness can become the straight path into your kingdom of unconditional love. Guide us by your Spirit toward the visions you set before us. Give us your peace. Give us the graces we need to bloom in your time and your way, in the places where you plant us.*

*We thank you Father, in Jesus' name, Amen.*

# Meditation 25: Simplicity a Key to Life

God calls us to lead simple lives free from worldly thinking and possessions. Simplicity is a key to life and true peace. True security can only come through faith in God, not money or material things. It is good for us to give away what we don't need and share what we have. Trust God, he is more than enough. When we empty out our baskets of plenty, we never run out, if we live in God and trust in his providence. When we worry about money and not having enough, we stay attached to the world and our own abilities, keeping God's hand from moving in our lives.

There is never any lack in God. When we live in the Spirit and seek the kingdom of righteousness, what we need will be provided. Lack occurs when we live in our own thinking, considering our own limited abilities alone. Lack is a state of the soul, a belief that there's never enough. This is not an economic status. A fear of lack can foster greed and hoarding.

When we live in the Spirit, we live in the center of God's will. This is a harmonic flow of giving and receiving. It is like a windfall of possibilities, where there is no worry about what we are going to eat, or how we are going to pay the bills. When we go with the flow of the harmonies of heaven, anything is possible. Pray for strong faith, free from worry; we can bring the very things we fear into our lives.

Living in fear about never having enough, is like crawling through mud and swimming in murky waters. Many are drowning in a sea of lies and worldly illusions. Many people who put their faith in money and things, fear lack more than people with nothing. It is amazing how people without jobs, money, or a place to live, survive, some with very little to no public assistance. This is because God is amazing.

When we live in the flow of the harmonies of heaven, we will experience exultant joy in life. In God we can experience fun and laughter. Keep pondering the great mysteries of God to find true joy in life. Enjoy nature and every season under the sun; in everything find the great mysteries of love and life. We go through seasons in life, enjoy them; remembering true joy and peace are present even in the midst of chaos.

We should give our lives to God every day. Release every situation to God and pray for direction. We should never let anxiety control and consume our lives. Focus on solutions one day at a time and watch God work things out. Watch and see the bounty of blessings and opportunities, patient trust fosters. Be at peace knowing that in God there is true security.

We should try not to control or manipulate others. Everyone around us needs the freedom to be who they are, and to do what they need to do as adults. We should guide our children to do what is right and just. Focus more on building good inner character, than on external success and accomplishments. Guide them and support them in moving toward their purposes in life, and love them unconditionally. Though it is good to share our thoughts and ideals, we should try not to force them on others. We should try not to push our ideals on others about how we think things should be. When we try to solve problems with our worldly thinking, we usually end up creating new problems. Everything doesn't have to always be our way.

We should try not to be too attached to money or material things. The more possessions we have, the more we become a slave to them. Eventually our possessions begin to own us. A lot of money and possessions can become quite time consuming. They can become our master. We should pray to the Holy Spirit about how to give and share more abundantly. When we give and trust God, we'll have an unending supply of what we need. Seeking a simple life is a key to freedom. Once we find this freedom from worldly attachments, we'll never have to worry about our bills or what we need.

*Pray: God of abundant life, help us all enter into the abundant supply of the richness of your kingdom of love and life. We surrender all to the Holy Spirit; show us how we can give more generously. Give us the grace to detach from our worldly possessions and thinking. Your kingdom of abundant life is worth more than gold. Give us the grace to give and share with trust. You are all that we need and more than enough.*

*We ask for a mighty outpouring of the Holy Spirit upon us and the whole world. Help us to step out of ourselves and into your abundant life, love, peace, and joy. Let all your people on earth live in the harmonies of heaven, where all our needs are met. You are an unending supply of goodness and grace; fill our hearts to overflowing.*

*We pray this prayer with thanksgiving and praise to the Father, Christ Jesus, and the Holy Spirit, Amen.*

# Meditation 26: Persevere in Faith, Hope, and Love

Everything starts with faith. Faith is not just a stagnant substance, but a moving creative force of power and light. Our words and thoughts move through faith. Faith is to believe in what is invisible to our eyes. Faith is to know all things are possible with God.

God gives us visions to hope for. When we wait in God for the visions he sets before us with faith, we grow in patience. Patient waiting builds perseverance. To persevere with faith, is to hope. When we hope, trusting in God's promises, not our external circumstances, we grow in love. The Word teaches the fruits of the Spirit of love are charity, faithfulness, peace, joy, generosity, kindness, gentleness, patience, and self-control (cf. Gal. 5:22-23). When we persevere in faith, standing on God's promises, not our external circumstances, we will begin to grow in the inner character of Christ. This is why God permits trials and sufferings; he wants to mold us and transform us into his image.

There is power in our words and thoughts. Let them be love, light, and goodness. We should give God all our worries and sufferings, speaking and praying God's will in every situation. When we surrender our adversity to God, write down positive solutions to each situation. Let these solutions rise up as a prayer to God. We should offer up our visions and concerns daily. Accept whatever God permits in our lives as a pathway to a greater good.

Learn from and look for God's hand in every situation. Always focus on the love and the light of God's presence; wait and watch God work things out.

We should seek the light of truth, to renew our words and thoughts. We have a way of moving toward the things we think about, and entering into the things we fear. With words we can prophesy our future; we can bring the very things we fear into our lives. God's kingdom is righteousness, peace, and joy. God is power, love, and a peaceful mind. To move and live in Christ is to live in his kingdom of life, righteousness, peace, and joy on earth, as it is heaven. This is regardless of what happens to us externally. When our hearts are transformed in his image, we will have greater charity and peace in the world. When our words and thoughts are fueled by faith, hope, and love, we bring a greater presence of light into the world.

The words that come from our mouths speak what is in our hearts. Let our words be life, light, and love. When we have thoughts and words of darkness, death, and destruction, we can bring a stronger presence of these things into our lives. Negative thoughts and words can attract spirits of darkness. When our words are fueled by fear and anger, God permits us to face the demons of our weaknesses. We should pray to God for his grace and strength, joining these things to the cross of Christ. When we die with Christ, we rise with him. This is dying to our nature of selfishness and pride, and taking on the inner character of Christ's life within. God waits patiently for us to understand this and apply this to our lives.      Pray always, with faith, for everyone.

Faith will carry us, as we wait in hope, and love will take us higher.

*Pray: Most High God of the heavens, mountains, and earth give us the faith to believe in all that is true, visible and invisible. We pray to have your miracle working power in our lives and in the world today. We pray for the grace to grow in faith, hope, and love. Fill our hearts to overflowing with your love. Let us bear fruits of peace, joy, and generosity. Let our thoughts and words be renewed in pure light. Sanctify our minds in truth. Give us your words of life, so that all of our words become Spirit and life. Let our prayers, words, and thoughts be pure and holy, so that they manifest as miracles, healings, and power throughout the world.*

*We ask this with thanksgiving to the Father, Christ Jesus, and the Spirit of love, Amen.*

# Meditation 27: Roses with Thorns

*"Like a Rose"*

*When Jesus comes to dwell in our hearts, our hearts unfold and bloom like a rose, with the sweet fragrance of Christ's life within. Like a rose, we still carry our thorns, for we are not perfect, as he is perfect. As we become more like him, our thorns are pruned one by one. He prunes us with his most merciful love. - J.A.L*

One of the flowers with the sweetest fragrance has many thorns. These thorns protect the plant naturally. God doesn't remove all of our thorns, because it is these very thorns that protect us. Thorns are our weaknesses. It is at times of weakness that we acknowledge him. We call upon him, recognizing our total dependency on him. This is how we grow. When we are pruned like a rosebush, we grow stronger.

We don't give our children everything just because they kick and scream, because it would spoil them. God calls us to be children with the inner character of Christ. When our weaknesses cause us to falter, we need to cry out for mercy and grace. We need to ask God for forgiveness, and forgive all those who have harmed us. Always be faithful no matter what; do not shrink back from God. He is always closer than we think; soon his grace will come flooding in. It is often in times of desperation that God's grace moves most powerfully. God is faithful to those who love him; he is near and with us even when we can't feel him.

*Pray: God of merciful love and pure light, be merciful toward us all. Forgive us in times of weakness, and help us with your grace to forgive others. Give us the strength we need in weakness, to endure all you permit to occur in our lives. Though none of us are perfect, you guide us to the highest perfection in the kingdom of love. Fill our hearts with your most merciful love, so that we may endure all trials, for the glory of the Father. Illuminate all consciences in the light of Christ, so that we all grow in the love and knowledge of God.*

*We ask this in the name of the Father, Son, and Holy Spirit, Amen.*

# Meditation 28: "Like a Butterfly" The Transformation of the Soul

God transforms us like caterpillars into butterflies. When we first experience new birth in Christ, we crawl from works to works, consuming as much spiritual food as we can. We engage in many works whether God leads us or not. We are overwhelmed in the joy and peace of our new found love. We have tasted the love of God, his goodness, peace and joy. We will never be satisfied with anything less; we will never be the same.

It is now time to enter the chrysalis of inner transformation, a place where God's perfect love and his pure light are at work. This is a secret place where our outer selves die and our inner spirit rises up with God. We wait patiently inside the chrysalis with hope, until God resurrects us into beautiful butterflies. With the light of faith, we wait in hope, to be set free on the wind of the Spirit. If we are set free too soon, we will suffer judgment, for we are not ready. If we are kept from rising when ready, we will suffocate under the oppression of darkness, living in a trapped existence of inner suffering, by allowing our feelings about injustice, to control us.

The chrysalis represents dying to our own selfishness, arrogance, strong will, and ways contrary to God. As we surrender into the perfect will of God, we will be set free from external oppression holding us back. In this chrysalis, we wait with faith, persevering in all the little

71

things he asks of us. In joyful hope, we wait for the day he sets us free to fly on the wind of the Spirit, in his way, in his time. Like a butterfly we fly, in the Spirit of peace, in the rest of God.

*Pray: Eternal God of grace and mercy, give us your grace to endure all the things you allow to happen in our lives with patience and steadfast perseverance. We pray that you deliver us from all fear, anxiety, and hopelessness, as we wait for breakthroughs and answers to our prayers. Build a kingdom of hope in our souls, and fill our souls with joy and peace, as we persevere toward the vision you set before us. Forgive us all when we fail, as we forgive others. Be with us, as we move and grow toward the highest perfection. Give us all the grace to taste the joy and peace of your kingdom of love, on earth, as it is in heaven.*

*We pray this for the glory of the Father, our Lord and Savior Jesus Christ, with the Holy Spirit, one God, true God, forever and ever, Amen.*

## Meditation 29: Focus on what is Good

Rather than fight against adversity, advocate the things that are good. The best way to promote what we believe in, is to become an example of what we believe in. The more we fight against something the bigger we make it. We have a way of moving toward the things we focus on. Fear is an obstacle to faith. We can enter into the things we fear. To worry and fear is to doubt God. God's news is Good News; believe in the works of the Spirit of light and truth. We need to trust God, not our external circumstances. When we live in God's love there is nothing to fear. Fear can be a warning from God. Pray for peace and follow the Holy Spirit's guidance.

God gives us hearts for justice. When we hear of something that is unjust, we need to give it to God and pray, asking God what he wills to be done about it. God is always bigger than our human solutions. As we grow in Christ, we develop hearts for justice; from the debts of our beings we hear the cries of the poor, sick, and the marginalized. We often shake our fist at the fruits of our problems while we fail to see the roots. We should ask God for the wisdom to help us see the roots of our problems and how we can change.

We need God's grace and healing to change. Laws alone can't completely solve our problems. Though we may solve one problem, we create other problems, sometimes bigger than the previous problem. Not everything that is legal is good. Laws don't change hearts, only God's grace can, if people are willing to change.

We have a way of complaining about the weeds in other people's gardens, while we fail to tend to the weeds in our own garden. We often look at all the junk cluttering other people's temples, while we fail to see the junk cluttering our own temples. God calls us to be pillars of light. He calls us to reach out to others with mercy and love. When we choose goodness and light, the light of Christ engulfs the darkness and crushes it. Whenever darkness and light meet, darkness gives away. God's holy light is always greater than the darkness.

Overcoming pain, insult, violence, and death, with more pain, insult, violence, and death increases what we fight against. Overcome pain, darkness, and suffering with prayer, blessings, and charity. We are blessed when we are persecuted for doing what is right and just. The Kingdom of God grows with even the tiniest acts of kindness, goodness, and charity. God calls us to be members of his army of goodness and light. When we choose God's side, we join the winning team. The victory has been won!

*Pray: Heavenly Father, through your Son and our Lord Jesus Christ, the victory has been won. Through his holy cross, he redeemed all of mankind. Christ's cross and resurrection are victory over sin and death. Renew our hearts in Christ, so that through his death and resurrection, we can be brought to new life. Infuse the light of Christ into our minds, so that our thoughts are sanctified in the mind of Christ. Infuse the love of Christ* into our hearts, so that we can be transformed into the image of Christ.

Give us the grace to become better examples of merciful love to a suffering world. We pray that all souls are saved from the pit of death. Let all souls respond to the call of God, to turn away from darkness toward the kingdom of goodness and light. Forgive us all, and save us all from the fires of destruction. God of mercy and light, be merciful toward all of us.

We give all glory and praise to the Father of merciful love, in Jesus' name, Amen.

# Meditation 30: Why so much Suffering?

God permits suffering when he can see a greater good. The path to God's kingdom is straight and narrow, but for many it can be a long and winding road of despair and discouragement. God desires that all his children taste his love, joy, and peace. When we choose the center of God's will, we can taste the joy of heaven while we live on earth. God permits us to eat the fruits of our own choices. When we make choices contrary to God's will, we can live in a trapped existence. Any happiness we incur seems to be fleeting and temporary, until we turn away from the things that are harmful to ourselves and others. It is only in Christ that we can have true joy and peace, even in the midst of trouble.

We are called to turn away from sin with true sorrow, asking God for forgiveness from the heart. We are called to turn away from all that we have done that brought suffering and pain into our lives, and into the lives of others. We need to forgive all who have hurt us and blame no one. We should ask God for grace and mercy often. Pray often for peace, for ourselves and in the hearts and minds of all people. It is good to surrender all problems to God, writing down solutions. We should thank God in all situations, even for the simplest blessings, like the air we breathe.

Darkness is part of God's creation too. He allows the darkness to come against us, and test us. Pray for God's light to surround everyone and everything involved in each area of concern. God's eternal light is always greater than the darkness. When God shines his light into the darkness, the darkness gives away. Ask God what he is teaching in each situation. Keeping the visions that God gives us before us, we are called to stand on the promises of our faith. He gives us strength, as we persevere toward the goals he puts in our hearts. Stay faithful to God no matter what; pray always and he will pour his love and mercy into our hearts. God is building hearts of love. He calls us to grow in the inner character of Christ. When God brings an answer to our prayers and rewards our perseverance, we become testimonies of hope for others going through the same problems and sufferings.

We are to help and encourage one another. If we all did this, great healing would take place in the hearts and souls of many. When others hurt, control, and abuse us, as difficult as it may seem, forgive them. Resentment will block the grace and healing presence of God in our souls. Not being willing to forgive is one of the worst things to keep us trapped in a world of spiritual darkness.

We should be an example of Christ to others, taking people to a higher spiritual level. Keep on doing what is right and just. Keep praying for people who are abusive. We are not at war with people, but spirits of darkness. There are people living in spiritual darkness. When we're the ones in darkness, we might find ourselves wrestling with God. When people try to control us and order us to do things, even when they are not our superior, look at it as an opportunity to be a witness for Christ. Don't be tempted to say, "Do it yourself!" Go over and above what they ask, taking them to a higher spiritual level. It is best to pray for them, and let the grace of God melt their stony hearts. When needed God can blast stony hearts, as hard as ledge; his power is like dynamite.

We are called to be courageous soldiers of the light. Christ has already won the victory. It is good to offer all sufferings to the cross of Christ. Christ has overcome the world. When we allow worldly concerns to overtake us, we can feel like we are crawling through mire and walking through sludge. Focusing on all the problems in the world and trying to come up with worldly solutions is exhausting. Keeping our eyes on the things of God, his light, and his love can lift a huge weight off our shoulders. We will feel the joy and peace well up inside of us. We will breathe easier, sleep better at night, and we will lighter on our feet. God will carry our burdens; all we have to do is pray and ask.

When praying for ourselves and the needs of our loved ones, pray for everyone who has the same problem. When praying for others in the midst of our own pain, we grow in unconditional, selfless love. This moves us closer to the perfect love of God. The highest love is to lay our lives down for the sake of others. Taking the back seat so someone else can take the front seat is humble love. When we give up time, money, talents, even our lives for the sake of others, we are transformed into the likeness of Christ. The more we grow in the perfect love of God, the closer we will be to him upon leaving the physical world. God is perfect, unconditional love, and pure light.

Suffering in disobedience to the will of God, leads to death. Suffering in obedience to God, leads to triumph. All suffering can be used to bring a greater good. As we join our sufferings to Christ's suffering, we learn obedience. All suffering is for a reason. Suffering is a test of our faithfulness. When we suffer for the love of Christ, we grow in love. When we suffer because of sin and disobedience, we remain in darkness, until we come to God with sorrowful hearts and ask for forgiveness.

There are many reasons for physical suffering. Our lifestyle choices can lead to suffering. Anger, fear, and anxiety can keep us trapped in spiritual darkness. If we spend too much time trapped in this place, it can make us sick. When our suffering is for no apparent reason, we should give it to God, and ask him how we can become testimonies of hope for others.

We live in a world with many trials and sufferings. Jesus gave up his life for all suffering, so we can be healed. When we pray for physical healings, we should ask God how we need to change on the inside. Healing starts with a change on the inside. It is good to include and pray for others going through the same sufferings.

It is good to write down our statements of faith, believing firmly that change on the inside will lead to physical healing. Praying for other's conversions and healings is an act of selfless love. The natural tendency, when we are suffering is to get angry, complain, and become depressed. When we rise up out of ourselves and pray for others, something greater takes place. Changing external circumstances starts with a change on the inside.

God's love is like a consuming fire that burns away all that doesn't belong to God. A person that has no love or light from God in his heart could be consumed in the eternal flames of God's perfect love. Salvation grace is God's unconditional love, which is perfect, and the pure light of his truth, which is his highest knowledge. A soul separated from God's love by sin, reluctance to forgive, and unbelief is a place of eternal suffering. This suffering is a call back to God. We are not to judge or force our faith on others, but we are to invite and encourage all to turn toward the God of eternal love and truth. People, who live in God's love and light, bear good fruit. People, who live in darkness and death, bear evil fruit. Pray for them; God doesn't will that any soul should perish. He continues to love us, even when we don't return that love.

Our spiritual martyrdom is suffering in obedience, until God's love is perfected in us. We will experience suffering in the holy fire of God's love, until all that blocks us from his perfect love is burned away. In this, we are proved in the virtues of faith, hope, and love, the greatest is love. Faith carries us, as we wait patiently in hope. As we persevere in hope, God pours his merciful love into our hearts. Love is our fuel, as it takes us higher in the glory of God. Love is more precious than gold. To stand on the promises of faith, as we persevere in hope, is the way of triumph through trials and sufferings. This is the way of the cross; the way of the cross is the way of Christ. Blessed are the pure hearts that see the face of God before their last day. All you who are pure of heart, you have made yourself ready; come and rise up!

*Pray: Eternal God of mercy and life, there isn't anything you allow to occur in our lives, which was not foreseen by you. Give us the grace to remain faithful to you. Help us to find the purposes for our lives that you have designed for us, before we were in our mother's wombs. You do not allow us to be tested beyond our strength, and you always provide a way out when we trust you. Forgive us for all the things we've done wrong to ourselves and others; be merciful toward us all.*

*Continue to pour your love and mercy into our hearts, as we persevere in hope. Give us the strength to endure all you allow to occur in our lives, for the sake of Christ and your people on earth. We offer up all our sufferings to the cross of Christ, for the healing of all your people on earth. Deliver us from despair, depression, darkness, and sin. We forgive all and blame no one. Let peace reign in our hearts and in the hearts of everyone on earth, including our enemies. Be merciful toward all, especially those who need it the most.*

*We ask this with all glory and thanksgiving to the Father, in the name of Christ Jesus, with the Holy Spirit, together as one true God, Amen.*

# Meditation 31: Lead by Example

It is not enough to say we believe, but to become living examples of what we believe. We all need to examine our behavior, and make sure we are not turning people away from Christ. God is calling all of us to prepare our hearts. We do this by turning away from sin, and toward a life in Christ. We all should pray for an illumination of conscience, to see through our spiritual eyes how we need to change.

We can't repent with true sorrow, if we don't see through our spiritual eyes that we are doing anything wrong. Often what we do in spiritual darkness turns people away from Christ. God is calling all to the center of his perfect will. The center of God's will is found by praying and seeking God's love and knowledge with the heart, not just head knowledge and external works of charity.

Sin is deliberately doing things, we know are wrong. People are in spiritual darkness; they don't see through their spiritual eyes that they are doing anything wrong. When we point out other people's sins, when we have sins ourselves, it comes across as hypocrisy. We should pray for one another and forgive one another, blaming no one. Where we are strong, others are weak; where we are weak, others are strong. We need to pray for understanding and wisdom. All people have a right to their religions, belief systems, and opinions; we don't have to convince anybody, but we are called to be a better example. We should not expect people to conform to our way of thinking, but should pray for God's transforming grace to change all of our hearts and minds. We are called to be living examples of Christ.

Jesus Christ lived and moved among his followers. He taught not only with words, but with example. He not only lived among his apostles, but the poor, sick, and the outcasts. Through his life he showed the way to his Father, the source of all life. It is our Father in heaven who chooses us, he draws us through Christ his Son and our Lord. Christ won the victory through his cross and resurrection.

It is through faith, repentance, and obedience to his will that he calls us to share in his victory. As the blood and water flowed from his side, he bore his church. As we drink from the living water of his words of life, we will have life. As we are washed by his merciful love, given to us by the shedding of his blood, we have the forgiveness of sins. When people truly believe, they will be truly sorry for their sins, and will receive God's mercy for the forgiveness of sins. When we are justified by faith, we are sanctified by grace, for the forgiveness of sins.

Together we are church; we are bones of his bones and flesh of his flesh (cf. Gen. 2:23), (cf. Eph. 5:29-32). He calls us to baptism, through the water and the Word. Through our baptism into Christ, we become one in the Father through the Holy Spirit. The Word and Spirit teaches, as members of the body of Christ, we are called to be walking tabernacles of the Most High God, and pure temples of the Holy Spirit (cf. 1Cor. 3:16). Christ is the head of the body (cf. Col. 1:18), and we are his members (cf. 1Cor. 12:12). The Holy Spirit is our lifeblood.

Christ our King didn't have an earthly throne like an earthly king. His cross became his throne of victory. Because of this one perfect sacrifice, we can have the forgiveness of sins. Because of Christ's resurrection, all who believe can have eternal life. God calls us to selfless obedience to his will. Obedience to his will shows our love. The more we decrease in our own selfish ways and increase in Christ's ways, the more we grow in the love of God. God prefers our obedience to sacrifice, but in our obedience, he calls us to sacrifice our time, talents, money, and things for the sake of others, with Christ's love.

Think about a field of sunflowers. Imagine how they grow and move toward the sun. Imagine how the sun's rays stream like swords of light toward the flowers. Imagine how the warmth of the sun feels on a clear dry day. The sunflowers provide seeds that feed people, birds, and animals. The seeds provide oil useful for cooking and skin cream. The sunflowers just are, without a worry or care. God waters them.

God calls us to pray for grace and to trust him. He invites us to turn our faces toward the Son, where food that doesn't perish is found. He provides what we need. In him we have life, peace, and comfort. He calls us to open our hearts to his warm rays of light. Imagine swords of light piercing our minds and hearts, illuminating our consciences, setting our souls on fire with his love. Imagine the seeds of the Word, coming to life in our hearts. Think of the oil as God's perfect love flowing in our souls. Through his love, God gives us strength, joy, and peace. Imagine the warm rays of light healing our minds, souls, and bodies. God gives us life-giving water.

We are called to be witnesses of Christ's life in prayers, words, and deeds. God calls us to spiritual worship with our minds, hearts, and total beings. He pours out his love and light, unconditionally. In turn, he calls us to pour out his love and light toward others unconditionally. He invites us to come to him with open, repentant hearts. When receiving Christ in Holy Communion, come with an open, repentant heart. Jesus is alive! He desires to pour his life into our minds, hearts, and souls. He desires to infuse his life into our total beings. All who are transformed in his life will receive the glory of the resurrection. Christ is our water bearer; he is with us always, until the end of the age.

True leaders lead through examples, not just words. God calls his leaders to be living examples of his love and knowledge. The love and knowledge of God goes beyond human intellect and emotional feelings. God's love and knowledge are an experience. We need to pray to receive his love and knowledge, from the heart. Leaders are called to reach out to the people, God entrusts them with. Leaders are called with a higher accountability than followers. People often don't go any farther than their leadership takes them.

If the mother bird doesn't feed her babies, they will not live. They need to be allowed to go out on their own to learn to fly. Let the little birds learn to fly. Lead with love, not fear or anger. The Kingdom of God is Good News. If all leaders would lead with prayer and the love and simplicity of Christ, more of the people who follow them would radiate the light of the Son from their countenances.

We should pray for our leaders, bless, and support them. God calls us to seek the spiritual things first. When we do this, we grow in trust that God will provide all that we need. His kingdom doesn't belong to the world. His words of life are our food, and his merciful love is our drink. He calls us all to be ready, clothed in power, righteousness, peace, and joy.

God calls leaders to be more concerned about the souls of their people. There is much concern over money and the external works of the church, while souls are being lost. Try to reach out to the people with the compassion of Christ. Their greatest hunger is for the Spirit of love and light. A lot of people have never tasted the love of God, or the light of his knowledge. They are hungry for truth beyond their human minds, and are thirsty for the love of God. Once people taste the truth and love of God, nothing else will satisfy them.

The greatest leaders don't lead by intellectual and political opinions, or emotional dramatics. They don't attract people to Christ by putting others down. They are called to reach out to people with the compassion of Christ. All believers are called to respect other people's religious beliefs. We are all called to become living examples of Christ.

*Pray: Father of the Eternal Word of life, you are merciful and all-knowing. You are far greater than our imaginations. Shine the light of the Son upon our faces. Pierce our minds and hearts with your sword of light. Fill our hearts to overflowing with your merciful love. Let your living waters of life flow through our total beings.*

*Let every person on earth experience your love and knowledge, beyond our human thinking and emotions. Help us to be better examples of the way of Christ, as we minister and witness his truth and love to the world. God bless all ministers and religious leaders. Send the Holy Spirit of love and light into their minds and hearts. Empower them to bring your healing and words of life to all they minister to. Clothe them with the power of the Son, to be your witnesses of Christ's presence in the world.*

*We give all the glory, praise, and thanksgiving to the Father of life, in the name of Jesus Christ, Amen.*

# Meditation 32: The Battle Belongs to God

Jesus teaches all commandments are fulfilled in the two commandments: you are to love God with all your heart, mind, soul, and strength, and love your neighbor as yourself. When we keep these two, we keep them all (cf. Mt. 22:37-40). Love is the bond of perfection (Col. 3:14) and the fulfillment of the Law (Rom. 13:10). God calls us to come to him with open hearts to his merciful love. He forgives our sins, and asks us to forgive others, as he forgives us.

God's love is unconditional, his wellspring never runs dry. God's love is higher than an emotional feeling. Loving and forgiving our neighbors includes our enemies. God's love starts with wanting for others, what we have for ourselves. He then takes us higher by asking us to give up some things that we have for ourselves, for the sake of others. This shows God we love him more than what we give up. What we do for our neighbors, we do to Christ.

God calls us to open up our hearts to his unconditional love and compassion; this is to be poured out toward others. God's will is that we all taste his love, joy, and peace and bear good fruit. The Word and Spirit teaches good fruit are love, peace, joy, kindness, self-control, patience, faithfulness, generosity, and gentleness (cf. Gal. 5:22-23). God calls us to show his love through prayers, words, and deeds. We should pray that God sows seeds of love into the hearts of all people.

The more we give love, kindness, peace, and joy away, the more we receive. The Bible teaches us that we reap what we sow (cf. Gal. 6:7-10). Generosity begets generosity; whatever we pour out comes back to us. The Kingdom of God grows with even the smallest acts of goodness and kindness. Wherever we are, we should pray blessings on everyone. As we ourselves grow in God's love, the world around us will begin to change, as we change.

God's love pierces our souls like flaming arrows. He calls us to overcome hatred, violence, and prejudice with his love. He invites us to pray, and become examples of his merciful love toward all. The Kingdom of God is pure light; his light is truth. His knowledge is above all other knowledge; his truth is higher than our thinking. He invites us to ponder his truth, meditating, with an awareness of his presence. Try to see God in all things, in every situation in daily life. When we open our hearts to God, we will walk in awareness of his presence.

It is good to ask God questions, being open to any way he chooses to answer us. Our own understanding of this falls short of God's ability to see the total picture. God sends the Spirit of truth, like swords of light, piercing souls and illuminating consciences. Through meditating on his words of life, we grow in faith. God desires all his children on earth experience his love and knowledge, which go beyond human emotions and intellect.

In the Kingdom of God, the swords of light, which bring us truth, and the flaming arrows of love, which bring us mercy are God's weapons. His weapons are not worldly weapons. We use God's weapons of love and light to overcome the darkness by doing what is good. Only God is good, so it is only through his grace, we can choose the things that are good. We have a way of entering into what we focus on, so that the more we focus on the kingdom of righteousness, peace, and joy, the more we move toward it. If darkness and evil come against this, God's light prevails all the more, making those who persevere more blessed with power, light, and love.

God's weapons do not belong to the world, but are mighty spiritual weapons of perfect love and pure light. His flaming arrows are the fire of God's love, which burn away the impurities from our souls. His swords of light are the anointed Word of God (cf. Eph. 6:17), which pierce our minds transforming them in truth. Our shields are our faith (Eph. 6:16), which protects us and preserves us. When we are hit between the brows with a rock, this is the revealed word, which changes mindsets and helps us to see through our spiritual eyes. Our helmets are our salvation (Eph. 6:17). To wear God's armor is to be clothed in his power. God's words of life and merciful love, transforms minds and hearts, into the image of Christ.

Trying to overcome adversity with violence and hatred reaps more violence and hatred. In God there is no darkness, only love's pure light (cf. 1Jn. 1:5). We should ask God to shine his light into our hearts and minds, to remove the blindness from our spiritual eyes, and reveal our thoughts that keep us from the center of his will. Christ Jesus establishes his throne within our hearts; his throne is his cross of victory. As our sin nature is crucified with him, he shares his divine nature with us. When we live in the center of God's will, we live in his perfect love. The heart of God is his perfect love; it is a crucible of purification and healing. As Christ shared in our human nature, we share in his divine nature, as members of the body of Christ. In this, we take on the inner character of Christ, as we are molded into his image.

Sin is when we consent to doing something wrong, which we know is wrong. We are called to turn away from what we know is wrong. Spiritual darkness is living in a way that harms ourselves or hurts others unknowingly. This is why we need to pray for an illumination of conscience. When we live in spiritual darkness, we contribute to it. There are people who don't know what they are doing, do to spiritual blindness. The light and knowledge of God can sanctify our minds and take the blinders off our eyes. Sin starts with our thoughts; the light of Christ can sanctify and transform our thinking, changing mindsets. When light and darkness meet, the darkness will recede.

We all need prayer and forgiveness; pray that all souls are converted to Christ's perfect love and words of life. Pray for peace in the hearts of everyone in the world. People will know we belong to Christ by how we love one another, bearing fruits of kindness, generosity, peace, and joy. Do not allow the enemy to divide and conquer us. We overcome dissension through prayer, fasting, and obedience to God's will. If we want to be respected, we need to respect others. It is difficult for people to respect all life, when their lives haven't been respected.

The battle between good and evil, and light and darkness belongs to God. Christ has already won the victory through his death and resurrection. When we die to ourselves and love God and others, we share in his resurrection glory. God invites us to share in his victory song. He invites us to become soldiers of the light, through prayer and fasting from our overindulgences and bad habits. We need to rid the false idols from our lives. These are the things that stand between God and us that consume our time and energy, keeping us away from the good things of God. The battle between light and darkness is Good News! The battle has been won for us; through Christ's merciful love and the light of truth, we will overcome. The two swords of victory are the blood of the Lamb and the Word of our testimony (cf. Rev. 12:11). Let all God's people on earth join in the victory song.

*Pray: Eternal God of perfect love and pure light, send your flaming arrows of perfect love to pierce the hearts of all people. Set our souls on fire for the love of you. Forgive us and be merciful toward us all. Fill our hearts to overflowing with your grace and mercy. Send your swords of light to pierce our minds with your truth. Sanctify our minds and illuminate our consciences; make us strong pillars of light and truth. Clothe us in the power of your love and light. Transform us by renewing our minds and purifying our hearts.*

*Renew our faith; we want to experience your love and knowledge in a mighty and powerful way. We want to hear your message, whether it comes in a mighty storm or a gentle whisper. Holy Spirit, come sweeping in and save us. Mount us up on the wings of an eagle, so we fly above the storms of life, abiding in your presence. In the silence of our hearts, give us the grace to hear your voice. We pray to hear your voice with the ears of our hearts, and see you with the eyes of our spirit. We desire to be aware of you in all things, and to abide in your presence day and night. We trust that you are always by our side, and we surrender all to you.*

*We pray this with all the glory, power, and thanksgiving to the Eternal Father, in the holy light of Jesus Christ, Amen.*

# Meditation 33: Love Bears Fruits of Peace and Joy

Salvation starts with faith in God. Through faith in Christ, God pours his merciful love into our hearts. He cleanses us from our sins and gives us strength. Through baptism into Christ, we die to our old life and rejoice in our new life in Christ (cf. Rom. 6:4). He transforms us from glory to glory by the transforming fire of his merciful love (cf. 2Cor. 3:18). In our love walk with Christ, he takes us higher, transforming us into his likeness. God is perfect love.

When we grow in obedience to God's will, we face trials and sufferings. We need to face the demons of our weaknesses to overcome them. All suffering can be turned around for a greater good. When we suffer in obedience, we grow in the virtue of love. When we suffer because of our own mistakes and sins, God allows us to suffer the consequences of our own choices. Our life in the world is a test; when we stay obedient to God during testing, God pours his love and mercy into our hearts.

If we keep crying over spilled milk, it will keep spilling frequently, until we stop crying over it. When we no longer cry over it, even if it happens, we barely notice it, because it has become such a minor bump in the road to true peace. The fruits of perfect love are joy and peace. True peace and joy doesn't come from a perfectly clean house, but is there even in the midst of clutter. Our faith grows stronger, as we surrender more and more into the will of God. To surrender is to trust God in all situations, beyond our own reasoning and understanding.

God in his perfect love calls us back to him no matter what we've done. When we come to him with open, repentant hearts, he will restore our souls. It is God's will that our self-dependency and sufficiency, becomes God-dependency and sufficiency. We should live in a way that if it was just God and our soul in the world, God would be more than enough. God's will is that we grow in the fruit of self-control. In order to grow in self-control, we need to fast from our bad habits and idols in our lives. Idols are the things we put between ourselves and God that consume our time. Idols keep us focused on the things and pleasures of the world. They can become not only time consuming habits, but addictions. We can become a slave to our idols; they become our master and control our lives. With the grace of God, we can be set free, through prayer, fasting, and repentance. Disciplined prayer and fasting from habits that consume us, through the grace of self-control, can discipline our sin nature.

We are called to encourage and uphold one another. God sends us people to help us, as we are called to help others. When we go through sufferings, we can become testimonies of hope to others going through the same problems. We can't always depend on this, because people are not perfect. The real test comes when we are called to face our giants alone. Our giants are challenging tests that could steer us down a path of hopelessness and despair. Sometimes God allows us to face our greatest challenges alone. Always trust God is near, and he never abandons us. As we are one in Christ, who draws us into the Eternal Father, we are not separated at death. We are never alone. As members of the body of Christ, the angels and saints are with us.

Often people with the greatest tests and challenges are called to the highest purposes, in this life and in the next. When we pass tests, we go higher into the rest and presence of God. Christ's church is one church. He has one family in heaven and on earth. We will see our loved ones who have passed again. We are connected through the Holy Spirit of love, life, and light. In Christ, we are one with the holy ones.

Perfect love overcomes the darkness. Love is perfected by obedience to God, no matter what we go through in life; for this reason, we have to face trials in our lives. It is our choice to stay faithful or not. To grow in love, we need to stay faithful to God no matter what happens. God is still near, even when we can't feel him; he is closer than we think. The more we trust and obey God no matter what we have to face in life, the more his love is perfected in us. We will have more true peace and joy in our lives. This goes beyond our emotional feelings; it is an inner peace and an inner knowing. To know in the Kingdom of God is to experience God's power, love, and knowledge.

He will continuously call us back when we fall away. We should always keep our eyes on Christ; he is with us. When we offer up our trials and sufferings to the cross of

Christ, we share in his glory. Every choice we make in God's will takes us higher in God's love. Our faith in God carries us through all situations, and our love for God and others takes us higher in the levels of glory. His will is to crown us with many crowns. If we choose humility, faithfulness, obedience, and perseverance in this life, we will receive crowns of glory in the next. Jesus wore a crown of thorns to overcome all of our thoughts that come against the love and knowledge of God. God calls us to renew our minds with his holy words of life.

In the middle of our trials and sufferings, remember the battle between good and evil has been won. God calls us to share in his victory through the triumph of the cross and resurrection; it is our choice. Christ's victory over sin and death is Good News. As this battle comes to culmination, the power of darkness will be broken off Christ's church. Christ will come again with righteousness, peace, and joy in the glory of our Father in heaven.

Love is the fulfillment of the age of the Law of Moses and the prophets. The fulfillment of loving God and our neighbor will be an eternal kingdom of righteousness, peace and joy in the Holy Spirit (cf. Rom. 14:17). Christ is our water bearer. The more we are transformed through God's love in the levels of glory in this life, the higher we go in the next. Christ our Lord invites all believers to come to supper with him (cf. Lk. 22:14-20). To all the faithful who respond to God's invitation with open hearts, welcome to the age of Christ Spirit, in the kingdom of righteousness, peace, and joy (cf. 1Cor. 11:23-26).

*Pray: Eternal Father, pour your merciful love into our hearts through Christ Jesus. Fill our hearts to overflowing. Sanctify our minds in the light of truth. Surround us all in your power, love, and light. Give us the strength and courage to remain faithful to you, no matter what. As we persevere in faith, standing on your promises, give us the grace to endure all things, as we move toward the vision you set before us.*

*Forgive all of our sins, as you shine your light in our souls. Transform our minds in the light of truth. Continue to pour your love into our hearts, as we walk in love. We pray that all of our choices line up with your perfect will. We respond to your invitation to sup with Christ our Lord. Draw us near to you, as we grow in the righteousness, peace, and joy of the Holy Spirit. Let us all be one in Christ Jesus our Lord.*

*We ask this with all glory, power, and thanksgiving to the Father of Eternal love, in Jesus' name, Amen.*

# Meditation 34: It is God who Calls Us

God's people on earth are the ones causing division on matters of faith. There is only one faith. When we put one another down, we put down Christ. When we point fingers at other's errors, spiritual darkness, and sin, while we fail to see our own, it comes across as hypocrisy. Instead of turning people to Christ, we turn people away from the very God who can save them. God calls us all to come to him with open hearts and minds to his perfect love and pure light.

We can only have true sorrow for sins when we know we have done something wrong. We need to see this through our spiritual eyes. We all need to forgive and ask for forgiveness. When we persecute and blame others, we are failing to forgive. This can be whole groups of people. Pray for them and ask for forgiveness. God is calling us to be better examples of Christ, as a witness to all. God's greatest leaders are called to lead by example. When we become a better example of what we believe, the truth among us will be made known.

God calls us to prayerfully offer gentile correction, always praying for the persons involved first. We should always pray to the Holy Spirit for help. It is good to write our prayers and solutions down in a prayer journal. It is always best to respect other people's views and understandings even when we disagree. We should never force our faith on people.

God respects everybody's free will, and is the one who determines accountability. The best way to witness is through example. Sometimes we speak out against the fruits of people's choices, when we might actually be supporting the roots. This is why God's way is higher than ours. Only he can see each and every person's accountability. If we are called to do something about injustice, we need to pray and reach out to people with the example of Christ. Remember that God alone is Just Judge.

Salvation belongs to God. It is God who invites us to dwell in his house. We are called to be a witness, not only with words, but with our lives. Pride is the cause of division; humility and obedience to the will of God, counteracts pride. Love is our witness; God calls us to love one another and pray for all. This includes our enemies. Only light can overcome the darkness, and only unconditional love can overcome hatred. God invites us to live in the center of his will. When we live in the center of his will, we have incredible peace and joy, even in the midst of suffering. We should always pray to the Holy Spirit about how to help others.

There are many ways to pray and worship. God sees and hears all prayer. He knows our thoughts. Some say or think they don't pray, but God sees when they are thinking about him. He wants to answer our thoughts, as well as our vocal prayers. He knows what we're thinking.

Sensory people want to experience God with their senses. God made them this way; he makes us all different. When we pray, expect an answer, though God might answer us in a way we don't think or want to hear. It is good to ask God questions. We should pray that everyone experiences God. Though knowledge starts in our heads, we should pray to experience the love and knowledge of God. Knowing God, goes beyond just knowing about him, but is about experiencing love, peace, joy, and life.

God allows people who don't know how to pray to benefit from the prayers of others. It is God's will to renew faith on earth. When he sends little signs, do not stop his little ones from coming to him. God blesses childlike faith. It is God's will that we respect all religions, and be better examples of our faith in Christ. Through our examples, we can make his truth known. When people say they have the fullness of truth, they should be good examples of the truth. God manifests in ways we don't understand. If we interfere with this, we could find ourselves fighting against God.

Only God is all-knowing. His thoughts and ways are higher than ours. In God there are infinite and unlimited possibilities. If people want to prove the mysteries of God through science, it is okay. It is good to remain open to the vast and infinite possibilities in God. When we limit ourselves, we will be limited. People in science should open up to God in his infinite wisdom and knowledge, to help them bring about advances that meet the common good of all people and the planet. God will help us when he is invited; all we need to do is ask him.

We are all uniquely made; we are all different. The Eternal Father draws us to Christ according to each ones calling and purpose. True unity doesn't come through conformity, making everybody the same, but comes through Christ, from the Eternal Father by the Holy Spirit. It goes against God's plan and perfect will to oppress the free will of others. Free will is a sacred trust from God.

Many people say they believe in God, but spend a lot of time worrying about their problems and worldly concerns. Worldly solutions alone often create other problems. We should surrender all problems to God, so he can make our wandering paths straight. God searches all minds and hearts; he reaches into the deepest recesses of our beings. He invites us to surrender all of our burdens to him with trust.

The Eternal Father draws us through Christ. The Eternal Father is a personal God; he desires an intimate relationship with his people. Christ and his church are to be as close as a groom to his bride on their wedding day. This is a communion with Christ and a spiritual marriage. We are flesh of his flesh. God wills that the body of Christ, his church become consecrated members. This is to receive the fullness of who God is, body, blood, soul, and divinity. God desires to have a personal encounter with every soul.

God's power is perfect love and pure light. He is not an impersonal energy floating out in the cosmos. Christ Spirit became a human being in Jesus. The Word came in the flesh in Jesus, and he comes in the flesh in us, when we invite him. He is coming again at the end of the age to bring fire and judgment to the earth, and establish a kingdom of love. God's fire is the purification of all that doesn't belong to God, transforming and building a new heaven and a new earth (cf. 2 Pet. 3:10-13). The kingdom of love is righteousness, peace, and joy in the Holy Spirit (cf. Rom. 14:17). He builds his kingdom and establishes his throne in the hearts of his people.

God is calling all to prepare their hearts through prayer, faith, repentance, and obedience to his will. If we respond to his call, we will grow in his perfect love and pure light. A pure heart sees God. All else will pass away. Trials and sufferings can be averted or lessened, through prayer and our response to God's call to change, except the judgment which is imminent. This will come upon us suddenly without delay. The time to pray, fast, and change our lives is now, someday it will be too late. Only our Father in heaven knows the day or the hour (cf. Mt. 24:36).

Jesus Christ suffered for us because of love. In perfect obedience to the Father's will, he encountered the temptation of every sin that comes against us. Though he never sinned, he knows what we are up against. He called upon the angels for strength. He is totally forgiving and compassionate to forgive all sins. It was through Jesus that God, who knew of evil only externally, experienced evil in the flesh, as one of us. Jesus shared in our human nature; he invites us to share in his divine nature. He is merciful to forgive all sins. Come to him with an open, repentant heart, and an open mind to infinite possibilities. God can solve any problem; all we have to do is come to him, pray, and ask. He calls us to believe with strong faith, and patiently persevere in hope, because of the love he pours into our hearts. In God's timing and in his way, we will receive an answer.

*Pray: Eternal Father, you are an all-knowing God. Your ways are higher than ours. Your thoughts are much greater than all of our imaginations. Let your ways, be our ways, and your thoughts, be our thoughts. Forgive us all for our selfish pride. Heal our divisions in your way, in your time. Make us one in the Spirit of love. Give us the grace to be open to all you call us to do. Give us the inner lights of wisdom, knowledge, and understanding.*

*Help us to understand one another with your unconditional love. Give us the grace to love and respect one another. Let peace dwell in our hearts and minds. Let every nation on earth know your peace. Forgive us when selfishness, greed, and pride stand in the way of your perfect will. Hear all of our prayers and answer them. Save all souls, and let not one soul on earth perish.*

*We lift our hearts to you. Baptize us in the Holy Spirit; clothe us in your power. Let all people be drawn to Christ, and let Christ be known to all people. We long to dwell in your presence, and to experience your love and knowledge in our senses. Send us your signs and wonders to renew and strengthen the faith of all your people. We want you to find faith on earth when you come. Let your miracles and healing power flow through us to bring healing to the sick and suffering. Let our testimonies witness your goodness and power, and let our words be life.*

*We ask this with thanksgiving to the Eternal Father, through Christ the Son, together with the Holy Spirit, Amen.*

# Meditation 35: God hears all Prayer

There are many ways to pray. God hears all prayer. God knows all our thoughts, and can see into the deepest recesses of our hearts. He invites all to come to him with open, repentant hearts. An open, repentant heart is a heart open to change, with true sorrow for sins. He calls us to spiritual worship. We are to worship him with our total beings, offering our hearts, minds, and bodies to him in spiritual worship. When God sees open, repentant hearts, he sees fertile soil. He plants his words of life into hearts longing for his unconditional love.

Prayer with faith connects us to God. It is God's will that we not only pray with words, but with our lives. In the quiet of our hearts, he speaks to us. Listen to his voice. Take time to be quiet before God and listen. It is good to ask God questions. Come to him with childlike faith.

Some people pray with their deeds; with compassion they reach out to others with love. Always give these deeds to God as a prayer. When we do our deeds with love, they rise to God like a sweet aroma. Prayer is not just vocal; prayer with the heart can be silent. In the deep silence of the heart, God prays in us. The sermon of the heart is greater than any sermon we will ever hear with our human ears. Though we learn from the written word and members of the church; the Holy Spirit is our greatest teacher.

When we offer our lives as a prayer, we pray wherever we go. We should pray with an open, receptive awareness to God's presence. Pray this way at school, work, and play. Be aware of God in every moment, and the Father in Heaven will pour out his graces upon us. In the Kingdom of God, prayer in the secret place, offered up to God unceasingly, creates works. When our lives become a prayer, and our prayers create works, we live in the center of God's will. When we live like this, we don't seek human praise and recognition, only seeking rewards for ourselves. The Father in heaven knows what we are doing and will reward us; his grace is sufficient.

There are many types of prayer; the first type is petition; this is offering to God our humble requests. The second type is praise; this is thanking God for who he is. The third type is meditation; this is thinking about the great mysteries of God's love and truth. The fourth type is worship; this is thanking God for what he does and everything he has done for us all. Spiritual worship is praying the mysteries of God from the heart. This is the living presence of the Word, flowing out from the belly, like a melodic stream. This can lead to prophecy.

The fifth type of prayer is praying with angelic tongues. This type of prayer builds up and edifies our spirit. We pray this way when we don't know how to pray as we should. The Spirit of Christ that dwells in our hearts prays for us. This prayer language can be asked for when we are baptized in the Holy Spirit, with the fire of God's love.

The sixth type of prayer is contemplation; this is when our inner spirit meets with God's Spirit. We move beyond the veil of the physical world, into the Spirit's presence. This is where God prays in us. In this place is the sermon of the heart. When we reach this level there is no going back, nothing in the world will ever satisfy us. All we can do is remain faithful to God no matter what happens; knowing without God there is total misery. This type of prayer goes beyond our thoughts and emotions. In this place the Holy Spirit prays in us; our eyes and ears of our spirit are open to the mysteries of God. God is revealing the holy face of Christ. We are meeting Jesus.

God's prophets not only have knowledge of worldly events, but see the mysteries of God in their hearts. God reveals his mysteries in the hearts of those he chooses. We enter into this place through God's merciful love, with true sorrow for our sins. In this place the more we die to self, forgiving all, the more Christ comes alive in us. God wills to illuminate all of our consciences, to show us the state of our souls. We will see ourselves as we truly are.

The seventh type of prayer is intercessory prayer. Once we know Christ and come alive in his holy words of life, we can intercede for others better. When we take on the mind of Christ, we will know as God knows, though not yet perfectly, until we are made perfect with him in heaven. The more we grow in the love and knowledge of Christ, the more effective our intercessory prayers become on behalf of others. This type of prayer prophesies the perfect will of God, and can lead to prayer breakthroughs, healings, and miracles.

We should not become discouraged if we have difficulty in prayer. God loves us all equally; he sees the desires of our hearts and fills us with grace and mercy. God invites all of us to come to him in prayer with faith. God hears all prayer; it is a right heart, open to his love that he looks for. We should seek and ask for our spiritual needs first, than our temporal needs. We should pray for all who have the same needs, not just for ourselves and our families. God blesses his people; he blesses us to be a blessing to others. When God's words become life in us, we are to become life-giving.

When meditating on God's words of life ponder them, asking God questions. Spiritually chew them up and sallow them. We should ask God to shine his light on our souls, so that we can understand his words in the light of truth. It is good to gather together with others in prayer. When praying with others, we should always pray in agreement. There is power in group prayer, especially when praying in agreement. There is strength in prayer, especially when we pray with fasting. We are called to cut back on our overindulgences. When we spend time consuming too much food, pleasures, things, and engaging in idle talk; we have less time for God. The less time we give to God, the weaker we are to resist temptation and sin. When we clutter up our spiritual temples with things and pleasures, we become spiritually blind; we can only serve one master.

When we pray in agreement in church, prayer meetings, and in families, we become active members of God's army of light. God's light brings down fortresses of darkness, around us and in the world. In agreement, we draw greater strength in Christ. When worshiping together with others, always come to God with open hearts to his love and light. Through, with, and in Christ, we are building unity between heaven and earth.

*Pray: Eternal God of heaven and earth, we offer you all the praise, thanksgiving, and glory. We offer you our minds, hearts, and total beings. Send the Holy Spirit of love and knowledge into our hearts. Give us hearts of love, and minds sanctified in truth. Make us all one in the Holy Spirit. Bind us together with your love. Clothe us with your strength and power. Build up a fortress of light to surround us all.*

*In the unity of the Holy Spirit, let us become a chain of faith, hope, and love that binds up the spirit of darkness. Let the holy fire of your great love descend and ascend upon us. Let the living waters flow through and from our souls, to bring healing, and the Good News of your kingdom to others.*

*We pray this, with all glory and praise to the Almighty God and Father, to Christ Jesus, and to the Holy Spirit, Amen.*

# Meditation 36: God has a Plan and a Purpose for Us

God calls us to live in him, as he lives in us. We are called to exult in him, rejoicing always. His will is that we find him, and seek his face unceasingly in the stillness of our hearts. When we hear the call of God's invitation and respond to it, we become active members in God's perfect plan. We are called according to his purpose, in his plan of salvation.

If we trust in him, he can bring all of our choices together for a greater good. Even our mistakes can be turned around for a greater good, for those who love him. When we wander off the narrow path of righteousness, God forgives us. In his mercy, he permits us to make mistakes, so we can learn from them. We need to think about what our sufferings are teaching us. When we wander off his straight and narrow path, he calls us back to him.

We are a witness when we become living examples of our purposes. We all have gifts, talents, and callings. Our purposes are what we love to do, whether we get paid or not. They are what we are compelled to do; they are our passions. In the core of our beings, we know. We should ask ourselves, how we can serve others with love. We can help others spiritually and temporally. We should ask God how we should help and give to others.

It is good to write down and list our talents and what we love to do. When we use our talents for the love of God and others, the fruits will be peace and joy. When we find what we love to do, we'll not only bless others, but we'll live a blessed life. Our lives will be blessed abundantly, with righteousness, peace, and joy in the Holy Spirit. When we live in the center of God's will, we don't need to worry about money, food, clothes, or where we're going to live. We don't have to think about money to have what we need. In the center of God's will is a flow of giving and receiving; we don't have to worry about our temporal needs (cf. Mt. 6:25-34).

When we seek the things of the Spirit everything else is added, for those who trust him. This is detachment from worldly things. Even if we live in a large family, we can have peace in the midst of the clutter. When we become overly concerned about money and material things, we will never have enough. No matter how much we have, it is never enough. We want more in this endless cycle of buying, storing, and selling possessions. We will never find true peace in having a lot of stuff. Life is a test, when we pass the tests, we will enter God's rest. This is where true peace is found, in the flow of the harmonies of heaven, in the center is God's will is love, life, and abundance.

*Pray: Glorious Father of abundant life, I long to abide in you, as you abide in me. I give my life to you. Fill my heart with your love and knowledge. Help me find my purpose in life. I pray to live according to your purpose. Draw me into the center of your perfect will. I desire to live in you abundantly, as you share your abundant life with me. Help me to be aware of my gifts and callings. Show me how to give, and serve others with love. Let all my prayers and deeds become spiritual worship, pleasing in your sight.*

*When you set the vision of your plan before me, give me the grace to wait patiently in you. I trust in your perfect timing, and the way the vision will be fulfilled. Be merciful toward me, as you teach me your ways. Forgive my mistakes and teach me, as you lead me on your straight and narrow path of righteousness, peace, and joy in Jesus my Lord. I ask this for all your people on earth; let every soul on earth find their purpose in the center of your will. Let the whole world know your everlasting peace and joy.*

*I ask this with all glory and praise to the Father of everlasting peace and joy, in Jesus' name, Amen.*

## Meditation 37: Seek the Spiritual Things First

God's kingdom is a kingdom of love. His love is like a crystal clear stream with no contamination in it. When his love flows through our human flesh, it reveals the contamination of our sins and weaknesses. We battle with sins, spiritual darkness, and resentment. Our sins can block the grace of God, and the gifts he longs to give us. Our unwillingness to forgive, bitterness, and anger keep us trapped in a worldly existence of darkness and disappointment. Bitterness can be deadly to the soul; it can rob our joy and peace. When we feel anger toward others that we choose not to forgive, there is a bitter root. We need to forgive and stop blaming others for our problems and the world's problems. To blame others is to judge, when we judge, we bring judgment upon ourselves.

We need to make sure that we are doing what we need to do, according to God's plan and perfect will. When we find ourselves angry, blaming, and judging, we need to stop and pray, not only for ourselves, but for everyone. When people are engaging in trash talk, gossip, and blaming others, as tempting as it may be to engage in this, it is best to stay in God's rest, and not get infected by their emotional anger and blaming. We will be accountable before God for every word we say; try to speak words of life, peace, and joy. Bless people with a merry heart and laughter. While anger, bitterness, and gossip are deadly; laughter, joy, and peace are life-giving and healing to the soul. A healthy soul can lead to a healthier body.

Spiritual darkness is a type of blindness that can distort our image of God. God is love (1Jn. 4:16), and the true image of God will lead us to righteousness, peace, and joy in the Holy Spirit. God is pure light; in him there is no darkness at all (cf. 1Jn. 1:5). God is a God of life; he calls us to live in his abundant life. Jesus died and was buried in a dark tomb and rose from the dead. Through faith, he invites us to rise out of the dark tomb of ourselves and our worldly ways, into new life in him.

Our sins, spiritual darkness, and resentments, keep us from fully sharing in the glory of the Risen Christ. He calls us to faith, repentance, and obedience to his will. He will forgive all of our sins, as we forgive others. He will then pull us out of the grave of spiritual darkness and sin into new life. When we seek his righteousness and the spiritual graces first, all of our temporal needs will be met. He calls us to trust in his providence. He calls us to give and share from our material wealth. We are blessed to be a blessing, and when we are a blessing, we are blessed.

God gives us many gifts both spiritual and temporal. We all have different callings, talents, and purposes; whether they are temporal or spiritual, we can glorify God with our works. We should never judge or compare gifts. We all need to be who we are and respond to God's calling. People with temporal gifts are called to good stewardship, giving and using their gifts for God's glory. Temporal gifts can be offered up as a prayer, pleasing to the Lord. Spiritual people, filled with Christ's presence, are called to be the lifeblood of the church. Spiritual gifts are to be given to edify and encourage the church. To not believe in spiritual gifts or spiritual people, is to not believe in Christ.

God is Spirit (Jn. 4:24). The only sin not forgiven in this life or the next is rejecting the Holy Spirit (cf. Mk. 3:28-29). A person who deliberately rejects the Holy Spirit, snuffs out all presence of God's light in his heart. We will know them by their works (cf. 3Jn. 1:11). Change and be forgiven, before it's too late. God works things out, for those who love him, and pray with faith.

When we find our purposes, we will know, and be compelled to do what we are called to do with joy. Everything belongs to God except our free will. All gifts and abundance belong to God. He gives us choices; choosing life leads to God. He calls us to generosity, kindness, and goodness. Our selfish, prideful, and greedy choices, lead to darkness and death. God sees the heart. It is not so much the gifts, money, and material things we give, but people giving and doing things for God and others out of love from the heart. A small gift given with love is greater than a very large gift given with vain motivations. All that we do is a prayer when we live in the center of God's will.

In order to live a life in the Spirit, we need to become detached from our worldly concerns, things, and money. If we live in the Spirit, we do not have to worry about food, clothes, and money. God will provide our needs.

When we consume our time, with worldly concerns, we will get spiritually stuck in the muck. When we live in the harmonies of heaven, we live in the flow of giving and receiving. We are called to rise with Christ, out of the muck, to a higher place in God. When we do, he will breathe new life in us. We are called to get in the flow of the higher spiritual things, where there is less concern about worldly things and a greater concern for the souls of people.

We need to get in the circular flow of giving and receiving, where there is detachment from worldly things, needs, and clutter. When we focus on worldly things and money there is never enough, but when we focus on God there is more than enough. The soul longs to be set free from external bondage, to fly high above the worldly concerns in life. When we live in the flow of giving and receiving, we won't get trapped in worldly concerns. We should never give to get; all giving should be done for the love of God and others. When we live in the spiritual harmonies, all we need is there. This is to live in the center of God's will, in the flow of the harmonies of heaven. Hanging on to gifts, talents, money, and things clogs our spiritual pipes; let it pour out.

It is good to pray and empty out of all of our emotional baggage and give it to God. We need to pray to be filled with his merciful love and healing presence. It is God's will that we become testimonies of hope to others. It is good to contemplate truth with our intellect and ask God questions. When we wait in him with an open, receptive awareness to his presence, he will answer us. Sometimes he answers in ways we don't think, and not always in the way we want. Be aware of random occurrences. He speaks in different ways. He speaks through others, nature, his word, and directly into our hearts. Sometimes he will give us an inner knowing, and we will have peace about it.

If we seek the inner light of Christ in our hearts, we will grow in knowledge, wisdom, and understanding. We will seek obedience because of love, knowing disobedience creates a barrier to his love. God continues to love us, even when our sin, darkness, and choices not to forgive, become a barrier between us and his light and love. He will sanctify our minds, when we contemplate his truth with open hearts. His words are truth, light, and life. God desires to heal our souls.

When we seek the kingdom of love with open, repentant hearts, things on the outside begin to heal and change. Change begins within us. If everyone would change on the inside, we would have less suffering and more healing. He clothes us in his power. There are many gifts to empower us to be his witnesses. These gifts manifest God's power to the world. He calls people to be instruments of healing and teaching. All gifts are given, to be used to witness God's presence to others. The most important gift we give is love. It is love, not our gifts that will determine our place in our Father's house.

The Word and Spirit teaches us the manifestation gifts of the Spirit include knowledge, wisdom, discerning spirits, prophecy, tongues, and interpretation of tongues, healing, miracles, and extraordinary acts of faith (cf. 1Cor. 12:4-11). These manifestation gifts help witness God's power, by empowering believers to be more effective witnesses of Christ and the Kingdom of God. Manifestation gifts give people courage, strength, and boldness. Through mighty works of God, we witness the inner virtues of faith, hope, and love in a more powerful way. Those who have these gifts are to manifest the love and knowledge of God. We are to show that we have faith through our works (cf. Jas. 2:14-26).

The Word and Spirit teaches us, the sanctification gifts are wisdom, understanding, knowledge, counsel, strength, reverence toward God, and holy fear (cf. Isa. 11:2). These are inner gifts from God, which shine pure light upon our souls. Holy fear of God is to know that when we make choices contrary to his perfect will, we can cause a barrier between us and the love of God; though he continues to love us unconditionally. Holy fear is to obey God, because we love him. Disobedience can bring greater suffering upon us than any trial God permits us to face in obedience to his will. Even though we face trials and sufferings when we obey God, we still receive the consolation of love, peace, and joy. When we feel anxious or uncertain, we should pray for peace, and God will give us peace. When we suffer because of disobedience, there is no consolation until we repent and seek the counsel of God. Remember always, the greatest gift is love, do all things out of love, for the glory of God.

We are spiritual beings having a human experience. God is calling spiritual people forward. We need to pray to the Holy Spirit about what God is calling us to do. He calls us to be pillars of light and truth. The bittersweet and sour fruits have become sweet, ripe, and juicy fruits. The butterflies are being set free to soar in the wind and under the sun. God is calling his people forward to the front line, as his army of light. We are called to make music, sing, and pray with deep passion from the heart, before the Lord our God. Music is a gift from God. He calls people who have this gift to bring life, joy, and healing to others. Music can fill a soul with joy. A joyful heart can be healing to a depressed spirit.

*Pray: Father of righteousness, peace and joy, you are a God of love, power, and might. Fill the whole earth with your love, power, and glory. Fill us all to overflowing with your perfect love and knowledge. Shine your light upon us. Give us the inner light to grow in wisdom. Let our inner light shine forth to bring hope and healing to the world. Bring healing and life to us all. Let the whole world know of your goodness and love. Clothe us with your power and light.*

*Empower us to be your witnesses. Let all who see us, see your reflection in us. Pour your Spirit upon us. We pray for wisdom, knowledge, discerning spirits, prophecy, tongues, and interpretation of tongues, extraordinary faith, healings, and miracles. Let us be a manifestation of who you are, and the great works you do, to the world. We pray that the whole world come to know you. We pray for peace in our hearts. Let every nation know your everlasting love and peace. Give us all the strength and courage to be faithful to the end. We pray for healing, laughter, and exultant joy, for everyone on earth, as it is in heaven.*

*We give all the praise, thanksgiving, and glory to our Father in heaven, to Jesus Christ, and to the Holy Spirit, Amen.*

# Meditation 38: Life is a Prophecy

History is important, it helps us see our past mistakes and prepare for a better future. Looking at the past can help us understand why situations are the way they are now in the present. Once we see how our choices in the past helped create our present situation, we can ask God how we can change to create a better future for ourselves and others. The choices we make have enduring consequences, not just for those around us presently, but for future generations. Change can happen when each of us takes accountability for our choices in both the past and present.

Each one of our choices in words and actions can leave lasting imprints in time that can be carried down through generations. These past decisions need healing if the consequences were bad. This is like a negative, residual energy that is carried down through the generations. We inherit certain traits that can attract spirits of darkness. When we make a decision to change, we can stop making the same mistakes and overcome the past; this can lead to a better future.

We should not dwell on past mistakes. This can keep us trapped in the mud until we decide to forgive and stop blaming others for our conditions. We need to have compassion and understanding towards whole generations, races, ethnicities, religions, gender, or any preferences different than our own. We're called to be understanding and sympathetic toward what happened to people. We need to stop thinking, "that's the way it was back then." These situations have lasting consequences until we forgive one another and reconcile. People have a right to their historical perspectives, but arguing over these things keep us swimming in muddy water. We are called to live our lives in the Spirit, change now, and move on to a better future.

People and nature today are affected by past choices both good and bad. The better the choices we make today, the more blessed future generations will be. Poor choices can affect generations of people until somebody decides to make a change. God's grace is more than sufficient to heal us now. Seeking God's grace to bring healing now can also bring healing to past mistakes. Forgiveness is very important in healing. Resentment and blaming others can keep us trapped in a place of continuous suffering. Forgiveness is essential to healing, not only for individuals, but whole groups and generations of people. It is good to ask for forgiveness for the actions of our ancestors and all those who have gone before us.

When whole generations of people act in a similar way, instead of just asking why they are acting this way and saying the things they say, we should ask God what he is saying. People not only prophesy with words, but with their lives. We should be careful of what we say, because we have a way of moving toward what we focus on and talk about. We need to listen to ourselves. We need to be careful we are not cursing ourselves, our families, and the nations. What we dish out in words and deeds can fall back upon us. Once God shows us our past mistakes, we need to ask him how we can change. He doesn't show us our past mistakes and sufferings so we can feel defeated or wallow in self-pity, but so we can learn from our mistakes and change. We then give hope to others going through the same situations.

God calls us to move, live, and center our beings in Christ. Procrastination is rooted in sloth and selfishness. We feel we need to be in control, when it is the very thing we lack. Do not put off Christ with excuses, finding other things to do first. God calls us to make changes in due season. Everything is for a season, a reason, and a purpose. When we are called to change it doesn't usually mean we need to go back to the old ways of doing things. We need to seek his perfect will, as we move toward the fruition of his great plan of salvation in Christ. We shouldn't let past mistakes keep us from moving forward in God's plans for us.

Receiving God's healing now can heal past mistakes. Mistakes can be our teacher, learn from them. Don't think of mistakes as failure, but learn from them, change, and move toward the victory in Christ. Shock culture can be a result of cultural hypocrisy. Instead of putting people down and getting angry, ask God what he is trying to say. Sometimes the message is that we need to change. We can be so focused on what others should be doing; we fail to see what we should be doing.

Jesus told his disciples not to throw their pearls to the swine because they will trample them (cf. Mt. 7:6). In trying to keep the pearls from the swine, we need to be careful we don't become the very swine, we are keeping the pearls from. We shouldn't force our faith on people who get angry and don't want to listen. Don't become angry and inconsiderate of other people's views. We don't have to convince anybody of anything. When there is resistance, pray for them. When God speaks, people listen; when we speak, people argue. We should ask the Holy Spirit for wisdom before speaking. We should respect other people's faith and points of view and pray for them. If we want respect, we need to give respect.

We shouldn't let our religious teachings become an end to the means. Don't let what we've learned become a barrier to truth, but an avenue to higher revelation in God. His knowledge is always greater and higher than our own. We shouldn't think getting religious teachings and scripture in our heads is enough (cf. Jn. 5:39-40). God invites us to seek his truth with our hearts. Remain open to God, contemplating all truth. Spiritually scrutinize everything, asking God questions. God wills that we all have knowledge, wisdom, and understanding in our hearts. When truth becomes life in our souls, it will begin to manifest in deeds, and radiate light from our countenances.

*Pray: Eternal God of unconditional love and knowledge, fill our hearts and minds with your eternal truth. Let your river of healing and love flow through our beings. Illuminate our consciences, so we can forgive all we have resentment toward. Let the words from our mouths be blessing, love, and life. Let your healing love and mercy flow through all souls to bring healing to the past, present, and future. Help us forgive, as you forgive. Forgive all of us with your merciful love. Release all your people trapped in the prison of bitterness. Make your thoughts, our thoughts, and your ways, our ways.*

*Let peace reign in the souls of all people and throughout the world. Teach us to love and respect one another. Let us all become living examples of Christ's life within. Shine your pure light upon all souls with great illumination, showing us all how we need to change. Bless us and all generations with your healing love and mercy.*

*We pray this prayer in the name of the Eternal Father, and our Lord and Savior Jesus Christ, who reign together with the Holy Spirit as one true God, Amen.*

# Meditation 39: The Communion of Saints

As Christ Jesus shared in our humanity, we share in his divinity. He transforms us from glory to glory (cf. 2Cor. 3:18). God calls us through faith to be baptized into Christ. Through baptism into Christ, we become one in his body (cf. 1Cor. 12:12-13). When we are baptized, we are sealed with the protection of the Holy Spirit (cf. Eph. 1:13-14) and filled with the strength of God, as we receive the presence of Christ in our hearts (cf. 2Cor. 1:22). As we enter into the waters of baptism, we rise to new life in the Holy Trinity (cf. Mt. 28:19). There are three persons, the Father, the Son and the Holy Spirit, in one God (cf. 1Jn. 5:6-8).

In baptism we die to the old external self, and rise to a new life in Christ. As we die with Christ, we rise with him (cf. Rom. 6:2-6). When we acknowledge the power of the cross of Christ (cf. 1Cor. 1:18-19) and the forgiveness of sins, we are filled with the love and light of Christ. For people who experience baptism or a renewal of their baptismal vows, the experience is a cleansing and a freedom from sin and death. In baptism, we receive Christ's life within. We become one body in Christ body, the church (cf. Eph. 1:22-23). We live as members of the body of Christ through prayer, the virtues of faith, hope, and love, and Holy Communion with Christ.

When we die our souls move into the spirit world just as we are. All that remains on earth is our physical bodies. In heaven we will receive transfigured bodies.

There are levels of transformation; each choice we make that lines up with the will of God, takes us higher in the levels of glory. His will is to transform us in the love and knowledge of his kingdom. When we respond to our faith through prayer and charity, God fills our hearts with his love. When we contemplate his truth and meditate on his words of life, he renews and sanctifies our minds. God calls us to be renewed and transformed with the mind of Christ (cf. Rom. 12:2). When we take on his mind, he will crown us with the light of his glory.

God not only wants us to know his words in our intellect, but to contemplate them and get them down into our hearts. He reveals to whom he chooses to reveal (cf. Lk. 10:22). When the Word enters into our hearts, it becomes life in our souls. We receive the Word of life through prayer and Holy Communion. When we read scriptures with open hearts, it is a prayer to God. Thinking about God's word of truth is a prayer. Don't just read the Word, but also contemplate his truth. God wants to reveal his mysteries in our hearts.

It is good to ponder truth asking him questions. It is the will of God to reveal the light of truth to us. He calls us to respond with faith. Listen to God's words, chew them, and swallow them; be open to whatever God chooses to reveal. We should ask God to illuminate our souls, so that we can understand his words beyond the literal meaning. We are not only to read and hear his words, but we are called to obey his words out of love (cf. Jn. 14:21, 23).

God sees the true motivations of our hearts. All things should be done for the love of God and others. We should never judge anyone's motivations, only God can see the true motivations of the heart. A pure heart seeks to live in the center of God's will. We all need to examine ourselves and discern whether we are seeking any selfish gains. We might be tempted to give just to get things for ourselves. God can see if a person is acting out of true compassion that comes from his unconditional love.

We are called to encourage one another when we are growing in Christ. God calls us to confess our sins with true sorrow. We need to be truly sorry for our sins to be forgiven. When we are truly sorry, our sins are forgiven, but our weaknesses remain. God calls us to pray and fast from our overindulgences, idols, and vices. When things and pleasures consume our time and we have no time for God, our flesh gets weak. Our flesh is our human nature which is weak without the grace of God. We have a sin nature. Without God's grace, we can become a materialistic and hedonistic people (cf. Phil. 3:18-19). We can become fat hearted, filled with the love of pleasure and money, rather than the love of God (cf. 2Tim. 3:1-4). The spirit of darkness knows our weaknesses, and will come against our thoughts with temptations; this is why we need to discipline our flesh with prayer and fasting. It is good to cut back on and eliminate the things that make us weak, and try to do a little better at doing the things we need to do. When God transforms us, the things that are not pure within us will surface and be exposed. He removes the weeds from the wheat, the dross from the gold, and the sour grapes become ripe and sweet.

Our faith will be tested; those who are faithful in small matters will be faithful in greater matters. If all someone owns is an old car, he needs to make sure that car is clean and maintained to the best of his ability. People need to do the best job they can for their employer, even if their jobs are temporary or not their career choices. If we don't have faith to believe God for small things, how can we believe God for greater things? If we persevere with faith no matter what, we will receive the highest prize. We will inherit the kingdom as sons and daughters of God.

It is God who moves us from the back seats to the front seats, for his purposes, in his time and in his way. If we try to move ourselves, we will be humbled. The choices we make that line up with the will of God take us closer to him; our place is determined by the state of our souls. The heart of God is a crucible; when we live in the heart of God all that doesn't belong to God will surface for healing. God's love is a purifying, consuming fire that burns away the impurities of the soul (cf. Heb. 12:29). God wills that our hearts become like pure gold. God looks for fertile soil to build his kingdom of love. He sows seeds of truth, life, peace, and joy in open, repentant, faithful hearts. We should pray for the will of the Father, and seek his plan for our lives. God knows what's best for us.

The more we grow in unconditional love, the higher we go in the transformation from glory to glory. We are to seek God's will above all else; this should be our greatest passion. We are called to be baptized in the Holy Spirit, and to walk in the power and presence of God. We are called to be his witnesses. To be a witness, we are to live our lives totally for God, as we walk in the way of Christ. To be a witness to Christ is to be a spiritual martyr. Our souls are tested until we bear mature ripe fruits. Witnesses to Christ bear fruits of kindness, peace, joy, and generosity.

God's kingdom does not belong to this world, but is righteousness, peace, and joy in the Holy Spirit. Rage, violence, anxiety, and fear do not belong to the Kingdom of God. God alone knows our accountability and is Just Judge. We are called to faithfulness, whether we are in a season of suffering and poverty, or prosperity and blessing. We should never pray for suffering or seek martyrdom. We have enough suffering without praying for it. We should pray for the perfect will of God and seek to abide in it, no matter what occurs in our lives. To be a witness to Christ is to be an example of Christ, faithful to his call no matter where he leads us.

The transformation of our souls can feel like an emotional roller coaster ride. When God begins to move in our souls, we can be up and down. We are ascending and descending in the levels of transformation. Christ's straight and narrow path seems to zigzag. God is doing a mighty work in us, continue to remain faithful. He molds us like clay, planes us like wood, and carves us like stone, as he paints his perfect image in our souls. Through this type of suffering, God is teaching us obedience to his perfect will. When we are obedient to

God, all of our suffering leads to triumph. Obedience takes us higher in the perfect love of God. When we reach this perfection, our joy will be made complete.

We are more precious to God than all of creation, and certainly he cares for us more than anything made with human hands. We are more precious to God than consecrated acacia wood, linens, and metals used to build and house the Ark of the Covenant (cf. Ex. 25:8-26:37). We have been given the gift of free will, we can choose to believe or not. All creation was made to worship God and flow in the harmonies of heaven. Through our choices contrary to the nature and will of God, we disrupt God's perfect harmony. The Virgin Mary, Jesus' Mother heard the word and obeyed the word. Look at her life; she is the perfect example of God's will for us. She did not choose abuse, violence, pride, or death. She chose life, faith, humility, and obedience out of love for God. In Mary's womb she carried Jesus, who is the Bread of Life (cf. Jn. 6:35), the Most High Priest (cf. Heb. 9:11), the Fulfillment of the Law (cf. Rom. 13:10), and God's Perfect Love (cf. 1Jn. 4:16-18). As the Ark of the New Covenant, Mary carried the Presence of God (cf. 2Sam. 6:9, 11, 14-16), (cf. Lk. 1:41-44, 56).

He calls us out of darkness to become consecrated temples of light. When we live in his will, we become walking tabernacles of the Most High God. He longs to consecrate us with his perfection, but he consecrates us to the measure we respond to his perfect will with faith, hope, and love. God doesn't give us more than we can handle with faith. Into the darkness, the fire of God will come like a thief in the night to transform heaven and earth (cf. 2Pet. 3:10). The time to prepare is now before it's too late. It is always better to believe than not believe. Whoever believes will not be sorry, but will rejoice. God wills to abide in all of us, it's our choice.

The Bible refers to three heavens (cf. 2Cor. 12:2). The heavens have levels of transformation. The lowest level is close to hell, and the highest is the perfection of God. Our place will be determined by how much we loved unconditionally, through faith, with the love of Christ. We can't earn this, we need to respond to God's love and be transformed in his image. Only God can determine how much grace is in a soul. When a soul meets the perfection of God's love, a soul will go to where it belongs. We will see our souls in the light of God. The time to choose to live in his love is now.

When we come to believe, God infuses his love into our hearts. We taste the joy and peace of God. Our souls are not yet perfect, so eventually we begin to face our weaknesses. No matter how much we confess our sins and rebuke evil, we still have to face the roots of our problems and our weaknesses. We battle between light and darkness, and virtue and sin. Our choices don't always line up with God's will, because we have a measure of spiritual blindness. God's perfect love is meeting the darkness of our imperfections, like a consuming fire.

We need to learn our battle is not against flesh and blood, but spirit (cf. Eph. 6:12). When we enter the battle between good and evil, God gives us the measure of truth and love we can handle. When we battle with sin, doubt, resentment, and other human weaknesses, we find ourselves wrestling with God. We have one foot in the kingdom and one foot in the physical world. We are called to overcome our reluctance to forgive with prayer, blessings, and love.

In the first heaven, God purges the soul from sin and darkness. We need to forgive all, so the Father can forgive us; he is merciful to forgive to the measure we forgive. We are called to die to our selfishness, pride, and vanities. We are called to detach from our worldly attachments. God calls us to pure motivations. We learn that suffering for disobedience has many consequences. It not only affects us personally, but affects others. This can leave negative lasting impressions in our lives and the world around us.

Through our suffering, we learn obedience (cf. Heb. 5:8). It is much more fruitful to face trials in obedience than disobedience. Obedience to God because we love him and others bears good fruit. We live in the physical world in physical bodies; there will be suffering. As we learn obedience, we still face external challenges. We are no longer subjects to the works of our external nature, as we live in the rest of God. In obedience, we have the mind and heart of Christ.

In the second heaven, we eventually see that obedience to God's will in suffering and trials leads to triumph. When we surrender to God and trust God, our love is made perfect in obedience to his will. Though there is still suffering, we know God is with us and will provide a way out. God is transforming us in perfect love and pure light. We take on the mind of Christ, as we grow in the knowledge of him. We are growing in the inner character of Christ, so our hearts resemble him. We understand, we are not only to believe, but are to be an example of what we believe. We are called out of ourselves and the ways of the world to walk with and live in God.

Our lives are lived for, through, and in God (cf. Acts 17:28). Nothing is our own except our free will. Our free will is a sacred trust from God. We follow the perfect will of God rather than the ways of the world. The world without God, is in darkness and will pass away (cf. 1Jn. 2:15-17). All who remains in God will live. God's kingdom has no end. All those that choose the way of Christ and the kingdom of love will live forever. When we choose to live in God's perfect will, we can taste the love, joy, and peace of heaven, even though we still live in our bodies on earth. The second heaven is a good place of learning and love. When our hearts and minds are perfected in God's love and knowledge, we will triumph. God is perfect love, in him there is no darkness at all.

In the third heaven, we reach the perfection of God's highest love. People don't reach this high level until they pass on to the next life with God. There is no more suffering in God's love, only light, peace, joy, and a life beyond our imaginations (cf. Rev. 21:3-4). In this pure light and perfect love, our joy has been made full and complete. This is a glorious place of unconditional love. Souls who cross into the light will taste this perfect love, before going to the place where they belong; a place prepared by God (cf. Jn. 14:2-3). In the perfection, we'll have the pure heart and the perfect mind of Christ. Nothing less than God's perfect love and pure light can live in the perfection. We'll know as God knows and love as God loves (cf. 1Cor. 13:9-12). Our transformation in the glory of God will be finished. We will be made whole and complete through, in, and with Christ. This is the throne room of God. We will rise with Christ through the triumph of the cross (cf. 1Cor. 15:57).

As Christ shared in our humanity, God shares his divine nature with us (cf. Jn. 17:26). The more our souls line up with the will of God, the closer we are to God. God loves all people equally and infinitely, but some choose to reject his love. Some make choices that snuff out the light of his presence from their soul. If people die with no presence of God's love and light in their soul, they are in grave danger of hell. People choose this for themselves. Through choices that lead to darkness, sin, and death, we can destroy the image of Christ in our hearts. If we repent and ask for mercy, God will forgive us and restore our souls to his likeness.

Our external beauty and success can't save us. Through faith in Christ, God pours love into our hearts. Once souls deliberately choose the hell of eternal damnation, they can't repent after death. The time to believe is now. Sometimes people who have external beauty and success, choose hell by deliberately rejecting God, who gave them these gifts.

People, who by no fault of their own don't believe in Christ, can turn to God at the moment of death. If they are truly sorry for their sins and receive the light of Christ, they can go to heaven. God is calling all to turn to the love and light of Christ, now before it's too late. Salvation in Christ is available to all souls who choose it. Only God can judge and see the condition of our hearts. When we repent, we can go from living outside of God's perfect will to living in the center of it.

Most people do not enter the highest heaven immediately after death. If we believe, pray, and seek to live in the center of God's will, we will enter the next life closer to God. The more we love God and others selflessly, the more we grow in the unconditional love of God. When we don't grow in his unconditional love and the light of truth in our earthly life, our souls continue to grow in the next life. God is the one who determines a soul's accountability. When our souls enter God's perfect love and pure light, we will go to the dwelling place where we belong in our Father's house (cf. Jn. 14:2). This will be determined by the condition of each soul.

When our loved ones pass and cross over into life in the Spirit, they become like angels and receive a dwelling place. They will have different functions according to the will of God. They are aware of us when we pray for them. If we pray for them, they can intercede for us better. Saints who are in the perfection have the mind and heart of Christ. They know the same way as God knows. They are aware of us on earth and can intercede for us.

Once we become members of the body of Christ, we remain members after death. When we die, we live. We are members with the holy ones in this life and the next. As members of the body of Christ, we are like a big ship sailing the stormy seas in life. In unity, we have strength in Christ. If we try to go our own way in our own little life dinghies, we might not be able to weather the stormy seas (cf. Acts 27:29-32). We are connected through our life in Christ, by the Holy Spirit. God is omnipresent and not limited to time and space. God's perfect will is the same on earth, as it is in heaven.

The saints in heaven with the angels of light are God's army of light. This army of light is a consecrated host. When we receive the Risen Christ in Holy Communion, we are being consecrated with the members of Christ's body in heaven. Heaven and earth are united in Christ. This is the communion of saints (cf. Eph. 2:19-22). We are one body in Christ, as he comes to dwell in our hearts. We join the communion of saints when we have Holy Communion in the Lord's Supper. Jesus summarized the life of Israel to perfection. The Mass is the highest prayer to summarize the life of Christ. When we are invited to the Lord's Table, we can choose to open our hearts to his presence or not. When we do, we receive Christ alive.

Christ's merciful love purifies our hearts and strengthens our souls. His words become life in our hearts and minds. Our eyes are open spiritually to the mysteries of God (cf. Lk. 24:30-35). If we choose to harden our hearts, we can go home empty. The Mass is for the living and the dead. When we receive the Living

Christ with open hearts, he becomes alive in us. As we receive Christ's body and blood, the Living Word becomes life in us by an infusion of the Risen Lord. As we increase in Christ and decrease in our sin nature, we share in his divine nature, and his human nature, which shows us the perfection of the Father. We are to proclaim the death of our Lord until he comes in Glory (cf. 1Cor. 11:26). This doesn't mean we need to act like we are dead. Jesus is alive! He's the Lamb of God, who takes away the world's sin (Jn. 1:29); our Exodus from the bondage of sin into new life.

The Transfigured Risen Lord, Jesus Christ, can walk through doors (cf. Jn. 20:19). He desires to walk through the doors of our hearts. He's knocking, we need to invite him in (cf. Rev. 3:20). His body doesn't belong to this world. God can move any solid object from the physical world to the spirit world. Even though we can't see it, it is still there. We could actually move our body through these objects that are in the spirit world, while we are still in our bodies on earth. At times God allows us to experience his Presence tangibly. Heaven and the church on earth are uniting. This is how it is when we have Communion with Jesus and the saints.

Think of the incarnation. The Virgin Mary was overshadowed and infused with the fullness of the glory of God (cf. Lk. 1:35). The Word incarnated in her flesh, in the fullness of everything God is. When we know Jesus, we know our Father (cf. Jn. 14:9-11). The will of God is that the Living Word in Christ makes himself known in all flesh. There is only one body of Christ; as members, we are one body, the church, as Christ is the head. Christ is one in the Father, as we are one in him (cf. Jn. 17:21-23).

Some souls need our help through prayer to cross over into the light of God's presence, do to worldly lives and attachments. This is a condition of their souls. We need to pray for the repose of their souls. Sometimes they try to communicate with us to remind us that they exist. This is why it is good to have days to remember our passed loved ones. Don't just think about them, pray for them. When we do, they can intercede for us better. A family that has one saint that prays is blessed.

When we cross over to the other side at physical death, we will not be sorry for the amount of time we spent praying. There we can intercede for our families and others more powerfully. Saints know as God knows; they have the mind of Christ. If we know in this life, how much more are we going to know, when we see God face to face? When we pray for our loved ones and others, and respect them in life and death, we help them.

Acts of love and giving not only affect our lives now, but can undo a lot of mistakes of the past. When one member of the body is suffering, we are affected. Pain in one area of the body can affect the function of the entire body. We are to encourage and uphold one another. We are to care for one another, as Christ cares for us.

To drink from the cup of Christ's blood is to receive forgiveness. Sin and a reluctance to forgive keep the life of Christ from flowing in our souls. This is why we need to repent and forgive to be forgiven. Unwillingness to forgive can keep us in spiritual darkness. Anger and blaming can become bitterness. Bitterness can become hatred, and to hate is to murder (cf. 1Jn. 3:15). This is why some people want to kill their enemies. Many souls are walking in darkness; we need to pray for them. When we forgive and stop blaming others, a weight is lifted from our souls. Bitterness is a prison, in order to be set free from this prison, we need to forgive (cf. Mt. 5:21-26). We need to not let our feelings control and trap us.

All saints come out of the murky waters and miry clay just like everyone else. God calls us to become saints. He calls us to faithfulness, no matter what occurs in our lives. We are called to have open, repentant hearts, with an open, receptive awareness of God. Faith alone without love is nothing (cf. 1Cor. 13:2). He calls us to selfless love. Through suffering, we are called to learn obedience to God's perfect will (cf. Heb. 5:8-9). This leads to triumph.

Our transformation from glory to glory comes through love. This draws us closer to God. He calls us to not only say we believe, but to become examples of Christ's life (cf. 1Jn. 3:18). We need to change on the inside. Change starts in our hearts. God calls us to the center of his will. When we live in the center of his will, we live in his love. God lives in us, as we live in him.

We learn about his will through prayer and the Word of God. When we pray, we should pray for all. With unconditional love, we are called to love all people, even our enemies (cf. Mt. 5:44). This is not emotional love, but goes beyond human emotions. This love cares for those who cannot and do not repay us (cf. Lk. 14:13-14). God loves us unconditionally, no matter what we've done or failed to do. He calls us to do the same. Trust in him, he cares for us, and is mindful of all of us.

*Pray: Eternal Father, you are over all of creation. You are mindful of us all. You make us and mold us into the image of Christ, by the power of the Holy Spirit. Transform us by pouring your merciful love into our hearts. Restore our souls. Through and in Christ, make us one, drawing us into the life of the Trinity, as one body, one church. Consecrate us Lord; make your presence known to us. Sanctify our minds in the light of your truth. Purify our hearts in the fire of your love. Strengthen and heal our bodies and souls with your perfect transfigured flesh.*

*Transfigure us Lord, in our bodies, minds, and hearts. Come alive in us Jesus! Transform us in your image. Move tangibly and physically into our beings with your Holy Presence. Bring healing to our souls. Let your living water flow through and in our souls. Let us all flow together in the unity of the Holy Spirit, with you Jesus, and all the saints in the harmonies of heaven.*

*We praise you and love you Eternal Father, with your Son and our Lord Jesus Christ, together with the Holy Spirit, Amen.*

# Meditation 40: Pray through the Gospel

When we begin to encounter the Spirit of Christ, we hunger for his words of life, and thirst for his overwhelming love. Our hearts long for the Good News of the Eternal Truth that sets us free (cf. Jn. 8:31-32). The Good News is the Gospel of Jesus Christ. Parables, symbols, and metaphors were used during a time of persecution and corruption (cf. Mt. 13:13-15). Today God calls us to explain the Gospel simply and clearly (cf. Jn. 16:25). When reading the Word, we should not only look at the literal and historical content, but ask the Holy Spirit to help us to understand it with our hearts. God wills that we understand with our hearts how the Word pertains to Christ and the Kingdom of God.

Faith comes from hearing the Word of God (cf. Rom. 10:17). Truly hearing the Word of God is with the heart. Whether we are hearing by what is written, spoken, or having tangible experiences, God calls us to listen with the eyes and ears of our hearts. We are called to offer our total beings in spiritual worship. It is good to incorporate visual, auditory, and tactile experience in worship. We are called to worship both emotionally and intellectually. When we worship and seek God with our hearts, the scriptures will be opened to us, and our hearts will burn within, with the love of God (cf. Lk. 24:32).

This is God's will for the church, to become like the Kingdom of God. There are hidden treasures in the Gospel for all of us who hunger and thirst for truth. We should ask God to illuminate our consciences, minds, and hearts, and teach us the hidden mysteries in the Word. The Word is Jesus revealed. It is God's will that we open our hearts to the Holy Spirit, and ask to see the Word through our spiritual eyes; take time to contemplate truth and listen for an answer. We should ask God to give us ears to hear his voice in the quiet of our hearts.

When God reveals his mysteries, they are worth everything and greater than anything (cf. Mt. 13:45-46). God calls us to pray and worship with our minds and emotions. Contemplating truth starts with our minds. In order to make room for God's love in our hearts, we need to empty out our emotional baggage. God is calling us to rise up and awaken to the higher mysteries of truth.

Worldly concerns, opinions, and petty human arguments keep us crawling in the sludge. When it comes to historical perspectives and literal interpretations, there will be arguments. When it comes to God and his eternal truth, he is the same yesterday, today, and forever (cf. Heb. 13:8). God doesn't change. This is why we need to pray and be open to God's love and knowledge, which is experienced. It is only in this place that we will know, because we know. If we think or feel we know, we don't know. God is stirring up his people to go higher into what the Word teaches us about the eternal kingdom of light and love. It is not enough to know about God. To know God is to experience him, in a way that goes beyond our human emotions, intellect, and reason.

Jesus prayed and prophesied not only with words, but with his life. Jesus lived perfectly the life of Israel, and brought to fruition the fulfillment of the Law of Moses and the prophets (cf. Mt. 5:17). The fulfillment of the Law is love. Jesus showed the highest love by laying down his life for all of us (cf. Jn. 15:13). The life of Jesus is sacrificial love, where he gave up everything he could have had in the world, including his life. This is the highest love brought to perfection in Christ. He calls us to not only pray with words, but with our lives. Believers are called to be a better example of Christ's life. We live his life through grace. His grace is available to all who ask for it.

Faith is like our ignition key. We can't start the engine without fuel. Grace is our fuel. Grace is God's unconditional love and mercy. We receive our fuel for our spiritual journey in Christ through prayer. Every choice we make that lines up with God's will, takes us higher up the road to the mountain of God. His road is straight and narrow (cf. Mt. 7:13-14). His road is the way of selfless love. Every time we become selfish and self-centered, we wander off the straight and narrow road that will take us to the highest heaven. We are called to love God completely with our total beings and others unconditionally, as God loves us.

In Christ, we are no longer self-centered, but we become God-centered. Our self-sufficiency becomes God-sufficiency. Our reliance on ourselves becomes a reliance on God. We are no longer self-confident, but confident, bold, and courageous in Christ (cf. Phil. 4:13).

Wherever we lack, God fills in the gaps. We realize all belongs to God except our free will.

When reading the Word of God, invoke the presence of the Holy Spirit. Reflect on, ponder, chew, and swallow his holy words of life. There is truly life in the Word. God desires we all fall in love with the Word. Christ is Spirit and the Word is Jesus. The Word and Christ Spirit have always been with God (cf. Jn. 1:1). God existed before the beginning of time, always, and forever. We should ask God to shine his light on any spiritual darkness in our minds and hearts that keep us from fully understanding the Word of life (cf. Jn. 1:4-5, 9). Though the Word starts in our thoughts, it will eventually take root in our hearts.

Once the Word and Spirit come alive in our hearts, a river of living water will flow from within us (cf. Jn. 7:38). The more we pour out, the more we receive, in the endless circle of giving and receiving. The Word flows like a harmonic melody in the soul. It stirs up our passion for the abundant life of God. When we lift up our hearts, expect to receive the Living Word. To taste and experience this melodic flow is to experience incredible peace and joy. Jesus is alive; he is a real tangible presence. The living waters of God are to flow within our souls and out into the world. Remember always, the Word is Spirit and life (cf. Jn. 6:63).

The New Covenant reveals the hidden mysteries of the Old Covenant (cf. Eph. 3:3-10), (cf. Col. 1:24-29). The New Covenant takes us to a higher moral standard through grace. When contemplating the literal sense of the Word, think about how it pertains to Christ and the Kingdom of God (cf. Col. 2:2-3). Also think about how the Word pertains to us. God gives us visions of hope for the future (cf. Jer. 29:11). We need to pray for a vision for the church. Things seem darkest just before a blessing. We should fix our eyes on the light of the Good News.

When we keep our eyes focused on all the external concerns of the world and the external workings predominantly, it can be like drowning in a sea of mud. Our heads may come up once in a while to get a breath of fresh air, but down we go again. This can give us a sense of being trapped in the physical world, where we're looking for the next human or worldly crisis to occur. This keeps us drowning in the lower level of opinions and arguments (cf. 2Tim. 2:23-26). Human reason alone without grace can cause divisions among us (cf. Jude 1:19).

Come to the center where Christ is (cf. Jn. 19:18). When we mock and insult one another, we mock and insult Christ. We need to pray, fast, repent, and come to God with our hearts. When we fast, we should cut back on our overindulgences, and cut out all vices that are not good for us. It is only when we are fueled by the grace of God that our works become true charity.

Without spiritual worship from the heart, the church will be dry. God is calling dry bones to rise up and seek the invisible kingdom in spiritual worship (cf. Ezek. 37:3-5). When we seek to dwell in the place of eternal life with our hearts, not just words, we will be more empowered by God to bring about true change. It is only in living and abiding in the Word and Spirit that we can have true unity. Christ reconciled all men into peace through the cross (cf. Eph. 2:14-18).

Many say they believe in the historical event of the cross, but they don't live what it means. If we truly believe in the power of the cross, then why are we causing so much division? Human arguments over politics and other worldly concerns, empty the cross of its power. We are called to die to our selfish, proud, and arrogant ways. Without the power of the cross, we are an arrogant, proud, greedy, and selfish people. The cross is a veil we must pass through to inherit the kingdom. It is in dying to ourselves that we find life in Christ (cf. Mk. 8:34-35).

The cross is the tree of life that grows in the garden of our hearts. Through God's merciful love given to us through the shedding of Christ's blood for the forgiveness of sins, we enter into his presence. The cross is a necessary key to unlock the door to the kingdom. He builds his kingdom in our hearts. In dying to ourselves and the ways of the world, we are crucified with Christ (cf. Gal 2:19-20). He calls us to perfection in Christ (cf. Mt. 5:48). The selfish, greedy, proud, people stay on the worldly side of the gap (cf. Mt. 10:38). Do not be part of the world's corruption, and all the things passing away (cf. 1Jn. 2:15-17).

It is not enough to say we believe, or we have the truth. God calls us to become living examples in the Spirit of truth (cf. 1Jn. 3:18). While we are still in our bodies, we have much to do. Though we still live in our bodies, our hearts can soar to the highest heavens, where we taste the love, peace, and joy of God. This is our empowerment as witnesses. This is our true spiritual food and fuel for our lives. This is not just head knowledge or emotional experience, but true spiritual communion with God.

While there are many storms in this life, God gives us wings to fly into his presence. It is here that we have rest for our souls. In the world there are wars, rumors of wars, storms and earthquakes. A believer's soul should be soaring above these things. Through prayer and fasting with faith, we can stop wars and change nature (cf. Mk. 11:23-24).

When we become soldiers of the light, clothed in his power, the spirit of darkness has to retreat. This is not worldly warfare, but living in the presence of God. God is calling his army of light to the high ground. We need to stop walking through the sludge and crawling through the mire. We need to be equipped for the culmination of all things. God is calling us to prayer with faith, repentance, and obedience to his will. When we do this the external things will fall into place. When the light in us pierces the darkness, the darkness has to give away.

People are searching for the love of God and the light of truth. Some people don't believe, because of the behavior of the people who say they believe (cf. Titus 1:16). Praying the Gospel includes praying with our lives. What good is it to say we have the keys to the kingdom, if we hide them? What good does it do to say we have the truth, if we lock it up in a box?

There are no excuses for bad behavior in the Kingdom of God (cf. 3Jn. 1:11). Bad behavior can snuff out the light of truth in a soul. The True Presence of God desires to dwell in every person's heart and soul. We are imperfect vessels. When we make a mistake, we need to repent and forgive one another (cf. 1Jn.3:9-10). God wills to consecrate us all in truth (cf. Jn. 17:17-19). When we pray, we need to go beyond our thoughts and emotions into God. We the bride, need to make ourselves ready for the groom (cf. Rev. 19:7-9).

Pray that all souls will be filled with the Holy Spirit. The dwelling place of God is in our midst, and in the hearts of his people (cf. Lk. 17:20-21). The church should manifest the Kingdom of God on earth. We have enough of the world, and its worldly concerns in the world already. Get moving in the Spirit of God, and everything else will be added (cf. Mt. 6:33).

Always give thanks to God with hearts of gratitude and hands lifted high in praise. When we do this, the life-giving presence of the Holy Spirit will flow from within our souls out into the world. Give thanks to God in all situations, in good times of peace, joy, and prosperity, and in times of suffering and sorrow. Thanking God during times of suffering brings down fortresses of darkness and despair, and builds up fortresses of light, peace, and joy.

*Pray: Almighty God and Father of the Eternal Word Incarnate, send the Holy Spirit upon the world. Fill our hearts with love, peace, and joy. Overshadow us with the power of your Holy Spirit. Clothe us with your power. Infuse your perfect love into our hearts. Send your swords of light to pierce our minds with your words of truth. Let the Bread of Life feed our souls with the food that never perishes.*

*Lead us with your rod and staff, (cf. Ps. 23) to the living waters, to quench the thirst of our souls. You share your humanity and your divinity with us. Surround us with the glory of the Father. Infuse the presence of Christ Jesus into our hearts and total beings. Jesus, come alive in our flesh. Heal our imperfections with your grace. Let your Word of Life become life in our souls.*

*Fill us with the grace we need, to grow in the inner character of our Lord. Glorify your church, so that we become holy without a spot, wrinkle, or blemish (cf. Eph. 5:25-27). Make us righteous temples of the Holy Spirit, and walking tabernacles of the Most High God. Holy Spirit, leap in our souls, and set our feet to dancing in the joy of our Lord. We rejoice in you. We believe in your promises. Fill our hearts to overflowing with exultant joy.*

*Shine your light in the darkness of our hearts and minds. Remove the stench, the darkness, and coldness from our hearts. Take the blindness from our eyes, so that we can see you with our hearts. Sanctify our minds and illuminate our consciences. Let the presence of Christ be born again in our hearts, and in the hearts of all your people on earth. Let every soul on earth experience the peace of Christ.*

*Let every child on earth be like an innocent lamb consecrated to the Sacred Heart of Jesus. Make your church a strong pillar of truth and light, so that she becomes a glorious light to the nations. We offer up our total beings to you Lord. Show us your will and purpose for our lives, so that we can serve you, with a right heart filled with the passion to do your will more than anything else. Guide us with the peace of the Holy Spirit. Wherever you lead us, we will follow.*

*Sanctify our minds with wisdom, knowledge, and understanding. Take the cob webs from our minds, so that we have the mind of Christ. Guard our minds with a crown of light. Make your thoughts, our thoughts, and your ways, our ways. Reveal your truth in our hearts, and fill our hearts with compassion. Let all hearts be overflowing with love for one another. Show every person on earth your ways, so that all will find their destiny in the Father's house.*

*Descend upon us Heavenly Dove. Baptize us, Spirit of Christ. Wash us clean in the water of the Word. Purify us as gold, in the fire of your love. Wash away all of our sins and spiritual darkness. We reject all the evil works of darkness. Fill us with the pure light of Christ. Give us the strength of the Spirit to overcome the ways of the world. Seal our minds and hearts with the fullness and protection of God. Come Holy Spirit!*

*Fill the vessels of our hearts with the Living Water of your words of life. Living Water of the Word of Christ bring us merciful love and life, so that your lifeblood flows through our veins out into the world. Move within us with your tangible presence. Living Word of God, we want to taste your goodness and grace. Let us experience your mighty and miraculous hand so profoundly that those who live in doubt of your presence say, "My Lord and my God!" (cf. Jn. 20:26-29). Speak to us Lord; your servants are listening (cf. 1Sam. 3:9-10). Help us to see and hear you with the eyes and ears of our hearts. We want to know you, feel you, and touch you. We want to experience your love, knowledge, and power with our total beings.*

*Heaven and earth unite. Let your kingdom dwell on earth. Abide in the hearts of your people with righteousness, peace, and joy. The Good News is our focus and our prayer. Have mercy on us, wash away all of our sins. Forgive us, and draw all of us into the light of your holy presence. Father, give us the grace to forgive, as you forgive us. Set us free from the stains of sin and darkness.*

*Illuminate us, transfigure us, and heal us Lord. Let us be light to the nations (cf. Isa. 60:1-3). Let all souls have communion with you as one, in the true unity of the Holy Spirit. We want to hear your holy voice of life. Help all of us on earth find you, and move into the center of your will. Transform us and transfigure us into the pillars and tabernacles of light and truth, you call us to be. As heaven and earth unite, let every soul on earth be one in the Holy Spirit, with the saints, in the glorious presence of our Father, with Christ Jesus our Lord.*

*Converse with us Lord and come fellowship with us, we long to be called to your table. Help us with your grace, to fellowship daily with you. We want to see you in the breaking of the bread. Bread of Life, infuse your tangible presence into us. Consecrate us Lord, with your most sacred heart. Be with us always, even until the end of time. Manifest your presence in our senses. Move us beyond our senses, higher into you. Sanctify our minds, with your words of truth. Make our hearts beat as one. We offer up our total beings as a pleasant offering to you. Break open the Holy Word of Life in our hearts, so that our souls burn with the holy love of our Father. We want to do your will with the compassion of Christ. Christ, you are our water bearer; pour your living water into our souls.*

*In our agony and sufferings, we call upon the strength of heaven. Deliver us from darkness and evil. By the sufferings of Christ, you know what we are going through, and what we are up against in this world. Have mercy on us all. Give us the strength to endure, and do all you call us to do.*

*By the wounds of Christ, we are healed (cf. Isa. 53:5). Every wound on your body is victory over sin and death. In our sufferings, we see the face of Christ. Reveal your truth to us. When we share in your sufferings, we share in your glory (cf. 1Pet. 4:13). Wash away all of our sins, and help us learn from our mistakes. As we change on the inside, heal our bodies, minds, and souls.*

Remove all of our thoughts that stand against your knowledge. Remove the thoughts from our minds that keep us from your truth. Surround our minds with the light of your truth. Sanctify us with the inner lights of knowledge, wisdom, and understanding. Crown us with the mind of Christ.

We join our burdens to your cross. Through faith you help us carry them. Forgive us, and pick us up again when we fall. We need your mercy and strength. Teach us your ways, we want to learn from you. We want to experience and learn about your unconditional and selfless love. Give us the grace to encourage and help one another in times of suffering and need.

Deliver us from the false illusions of the ways of the world, and the illusion of our false external self. We lay all of our emotional baggage down at your feet. We pray for the conversion of all people living in sin and darkness. Fill all hearts with love, peace, and joy. You have won the victory, Christ Jesus. The victory is yours. Let the whole earth sing your victory song. Let your living water and merciful love, which flows forth from your heart bring new birth and new life to your church. We thirst for your perfect love, and pure light, and we drink.

Even though we suffer for a while with you, we want to see the glory of your resurrection. Move in us in a way that we shake up the world with your power and glory. Rise up in us Christ Jesus, so that we manifest the works that you did in a mighty and powerful way. Lift us up from the grave of darkness and death, and plant our *feet on the rock of revelation and truth. We want to know you and experience you in our senses, minds, and hearts.*

*Come in the clouds of the Holy Spirit, with the mysteries of faith. Come with your angels and the mystical body of Christ on high. We want to sing your praises, with the angels and saints in the harmonies of heaven. Let your church be caught up in you, in rapturous joy. Set our feet to dancing in a new jubilee. Delight in us, as we delight in you.*

*We believe for a mighty outpouring of the Holy Spirit. Let tongues of fire dance over our heads. Come sweeping in, with the wind of the Spirit and the rushing sound of angel's wings. Let your people prophesy, have visions, and dream dreams. Move us toward the visions you set before us. Restore us as one, as you are one, Father, Son, and Holy Spirit. Most Holy Trinity, give us extraordinary faith, healings, and miracles. All things are possible with you. Let all people know that you are our God and we are your people.*

*We hear a voice in the wilderness, the one caught up with God. We prepare our hearts for you Lord. Make our long and winding roads straight. The seed of the woman has struck the head of the serpent (cf. Gen. 3:15). Let the prayer chain of your little ones help bind him up. With the Word of God and the Spirit of love, in victory we sing, our redemption is here. The kingdom is here. Let all see the Salvation of God.*

*We pray this with all glory and thanksgiving to the Father, Our Lord Jesus Christ, with the Holy Spirit, together as one true God. We wait joyously with faith and hope for the coming of our Savior, our Lord Jesus Christ, Amen.*

# Epilogue

The greatest desire of the human heart is for the love of God, in which we can be satisfied with nothing less. All else is fleeting. Though we may be happy for a little while, soon the newness will wear off, and we'll be searching for something else. My prayer is that all souls will come to God, and experience the peace and joy of his perfect love and pure light. I pray that all people on earth find this freedom in Christ Jesus. Let the Holy Spirit of love and light fill the hearts of everyone, forever and ever, in every generation. God bless you all.

*"I am Free"*

*Hear the cry from the grave, in the darkness of the world's illusion.*

*From the depths of my soul, truth cries out for truth.*

*From the depths of this illusion, my heart cries set me free!*

*He suffered and died, so I could be free from the chains and bondage of this false external self.*

*The tomb is empty. The Light of the World was born, has died, and is risen.*

*Now I cry, "I am free!"*    J.A L.

*"A Prayer of Thanks and Praise"*

*All Praise and glory belong to you Almighty God and Father, and to the Son, our Lord and Savior Jesus Christ, and to the Holy Spirit, the giver of life, who teaches us what we have to know, our greatest teacher. We praise and thank you for the rising sun, the air we breathe, the earth, sea, and sky, and all things created. We thank you for all the spiritual and temporal blessings you provide us with; we offer them to you with praise, for your glory. We thank you for your written word, which inspires us, and the spoken word, spoken by your faithful servants on earth. Thank you for the presence of your Living Word that illuminates us, and brings great life to our souls. We drink of it with great gratitude; it quenches our thirst. We praise you for your unconditional love and mercy, and the forgiveness of our sins.*

*Thank you for sharing your abundant life and the great bounty of your kingdom on earth, as it is in heaven. Thank you for the eternal life that we receive through faith in your life, death, and resurrection. Thank you for your Bread of Life that comes down from heaven for the life of our souls. We praise you for the burning love in our hearts, and the knowledge of your mysteries given to us in the breaking of the bread. Thank you for clothing us in the power of your Spirit of love and knowledge; that we may be your witnesses throughout the world. Thank You for all the wonderful healings, prayer breakthroughs, and miracles in our lives. Most of all, thank you for loving the world so much that you gave up your only begotten Son, so that whoever believes in him will not perish , but have eternal life (Jn. 3:16), in your house forever and ever.*

*We give all the praise, glory, and thanksgiving to the Father, Son, and Holy Spirit, alleluia, alleluia, alleluia, with jubilant rejoicing, Amen.*

Illumination is a meditation and prayer book about preparation and change. It begins with an introduction to prayer with the heart, and culminates with more profound mysteries of the Word and Spirit. It is written simply, to help all believers understand the healing presence in the perfect love and pure light of Christ. It is a message of the heart.

Julie Ann Lynch is a wife and mother of three sons. She lives in central Maine with her husband and youngest son.